No Way to Run

Caitlin Press Inc.
8100 Alderwood Road,
Halfmoon Bay, BC V0N 1Y1
www.caitlin-press.com

Text and cover design by Vici Johnstone
Edited by Barbara Pulling
Cover image Lucas Neasi. Sourced from UNsplash under Creative Commons License Zero
Printed in Canada

In consideration of privacy, some names and identities have been changed or omitted.

Caitlin Press Inc. acknowledges the Government of Canada, the Canada Council for the Arts, and the British Columbia Arts Council for their financial support for our publishing program.

Library and Archives Canada Cataloguing in Publication

Crichton, Holly, author
    No way to run : a mother and son story of surviving abuse / Holly Crichton.

Issued in print and electronic formats.
ISBN 978-1-987915-18-1 (paperback).—ISBN 978-1-987915-25-9 (ebook)

    1. Crichton, Holly. 2. Crichton, Mat—Trials, litigation, etc. 3. Victims of family violence—Alberta—Biography. 4. Trials (Manslaughter)—Alberta. I. Title.

HV6626.23.C3C75 2016   362.82'92097123   C2016-903264-7
                                                    C2016-903265-5

No Way to Run

A Mother and Son Story of Surviving Abuse

HOLLY CRICHTON

CAITLIN PRESS

Dedicated to everyone who believes that decency and dignity matter.

CHAPTER 1

SANDY'S BELLOWING WOKE me from a sound sleep, despite the audio book droning through my headphones and the feather pillow tucked snugly over my eyes and ears. The walls of our house did little to muffle his shouts.

Caught between sleep and wakefulness, I was swamped by terror. Always the same nightmare: I was trying to escape but unable to move. My shoulders pinched tight as I waited for the inevitable club-of-a-hand to slam onto my back, grab my hair or my jacket, and jerk me down.

In a panic, I flung the pillow off my eyes, pulled the headphones away, and pushed the covers back. The yelling continued. It was no nightmare. I could make out every swear word.

Attempting to bound up, I came fully awake, remembering I truly could not move my legs, or run, or get away. My brain commanded me to bolt upright. To dash outside to see what was happening. But my paralyzed body had different plans.

Sandy wasn't in the house, and it wasn't me he was screaming at, so I knew our son Matthew must be getting it. He and I were the two people my husband reserved his most violent rages for.

Gripping the edge of the mattress with my left hand, I reached my right elbow beneath me and tried to shove myself upward. The attempt at speed, as it always did, threw me into a rigid spasm. Stalled by my frozen body, I waited for the spasm to subside, then methodically pulled myself to a sitting position. Finally upright, balanced by gripping the bedsheet with my right hand, I used my left hand to shuffle my dead-weight legs around and slide them over the edge of the bed. Balancing on my right hand, I grabbed my sliding board from where I had left it and placed it like a bridge between bed and wheelchair.

Then I wedged the board beneath my emaciated butt cheeks and slid myself over.

Finally on my chair, nerves crackling with fear, I raced to look out the glass patio doors to see what was going on.

As I took in the scene at a glance, anger replaced my fear. I could see that Mat wasn't injured, at least not yet. For the moment, he was safely out of the reach of his tantrum-throwing father. But Sandy had cocked his arm and he was darting toward our son, prepared to launch the hammer he had in his hand.

My wheelchair wouldn't fit through our sliding patio doors, so I wheeled through the main entry door out onto the deck. I could see our white Ford Ranger pickup parked in front of the machine shop, about a hundred metres away, with a solar cattle-watering system partly loaded on the truck box. The water tank was on properly, but a solar panel was tilted half on and half off the end gate. It had obviously fallen or been dropped.

Sandy's shrieking blurred into one foul roar of senseless obscenity. Crying by now, Mat yelled back at his dad, his words slurred, "Why do you have to be like this! Why can't we ever just do a job without you hitting and cursing me? What makes you so crazy?"

His bum right leg dragging, his right arm curled against his slim body, Mat buckled at the knees as Sandy lunged at him. Feinting to the right, he nearly fell, but he managed to keep his balance and his distance. Clenching my teeth, I prayed, *Come on, Matti. Get out of there. Don't let him catch you.*

"You little fucker," Sandy bellowed. "Come back here and call me crazy. You don't have the guts to, do you?"

I clanged my wheelchair against the metal deck railing so they'd hear me and know I was watching. Sandy's head snapped around. He dropped the hammer he was holding and stalked toward the house. My stomach churned as I wondered if I was next in line. Maybe he'd throw me off the deck like he'd been threatening lately.

As he walked through the yard gate, Sandy looked up at me and snarled, "Fucking little pansy. Someday he's gonna push me too far!"

"He's right, you know. You do act crazy," I said in a deliberately non-confrontational tone. "I don't know what gets into you. How you can get so mad over nothing."

I looked down from my perch on the deck, gambling he wouldn't go through the effort of charging up the stairs to catch me.

"You'll see how crazy I am someday," Sandy yelled. "One of these times you and the suckie boy are gonna push me over the edge. That little prick always has to question me. I'm the bull of the woods around here. He couldn't harrow what I plow. You guys would be nothing without me!"

Sandy was close to tears, and I knew not to push him any further. I said in a soothing voice, the kind I used on a dog or a horse that was freaking out, "I know it can be frustrating working with Matthew sometimes, but it's not his fault he's slow. He can't help that he's brain-damaged. He doesn't try to be that way."

"You never take my side, do you?" he shouted. "It's always the poor little retard you stick up for. But you're Holle*eee*. You're *soooo* wonderful. You're *toooo* good for me."

His tone shifted from whiney to harsh. "It's no wonder no one likes you. You'll never have as many friends as me. Will you? Huh? Huh?" He stood at the foot of the stairs, legs braced and fists clenched at his sides, ready to spring up and grab me. Since he'd had his knee replacement, a little barrier like a set of stairs wasn't going to prevent him from attacking me.

Having to be phony was one of the hardest parts of living with Sandy. Agreeing with him in a situation like this went against everything in me.

"You're right. You have more friends," I answered in a flat voice, like I had a thousand times before.

As he turned abruptly toward the entry door downstairs, I rolled back into the kitchen. I could hear him start up the basement stairs. I didn't want to get cornered, so I rolled onto my elevator, quickly pulled the door closed behind me, and headed down to the bottom floor of the house, where my power wheelchair was parked.

The house shuddered as Sandy's 230 pounds fell into his recliner chair in the living room above. The television started blaring. At least I knew where he was now. He'd probably be there for the rest of the afternoon. He could watch TV for hours on end, crying openly over sad episodes and exploding with anger when he watched anyone being bullied. "That son of a bitch!" he'd shout, "I'd like to kick the shit out of him. If there's one thing I can't stand, it's a bully!"

CHAPTER 2

WHEN MY ELEVATOR reached the basement I rolled off, transferred to my power chair, drove back onto the elevator, got up to garage level, and headed outside. I turned our border collies, Zeke, Lady, and Tank, loose from their kennels, and headed over toward the shop with the dogs running ahead of me. Mat was loading the fallen solar panel onto the Ranger when I got there.

I glanced toward the house where Sandy was. "Was there a reason for that?"

Mat finished loading the panel, then stopped and rubbed the dogs' bellies one by one, giving his dog, Tank, a special hug before he answered me.

"I asked him if we could rig up a trailer for the solar water supplies," he said in his slow drawl. "He flipped into a rage and smacked me in the head. Screaming at me to mind my own goddamn business."

My heart clenched. "Oh, for Christ's sake. I'm sorry, Matti. I don't understand what goes through his head. But it only makes him worse if I try to talk to him about it. Then he'll take it out on you even more."

"I know," Mat choked out. "And we still have to finish setting up the water system. I hate it when I have to watch out for him and try to do my work at the same time."

"You know," I said to my son as I had many times before, "we can leave here. We don't have to stay. We can go to your grandparents' place in Valemount and live there."

"Mom. We both love the farm. I can't imagine living anywhere else. This is my home."

From the time he was small, Mat had wanted to be a farmer, not a firefighter, a TV star, or a doctor, like the other kids in his class. Even as a toddler he'd explored every acre of our farm, and he was attached to the land with an intensity few people could imagine. For the first thirteen years of his life, up until the time of my injury, he and his older brother, Jason, had spent much of their time helping me with farm work and training racehorses. The three of us worked hard together and depended on each other. For several months of each year, the boys and I had been alone on the farm while Sandy was away at a racetrack somewhere, running our stable of horses.

"Yes, this is our home," I said to Mat. "We will be okay. Just put your father's behaviour off in a corner where it belongs and ignore it. It's his problem, not yours."

I could see Matti starting to relax a bit. Even though I felt rotten about what had just happened, I did what I always had: I forced myself to move away from the darkness Sandy created.

"When you get this water system loaded, let's go work the dogs, okay?"

I watched him put the rest of the parts in the truck. Then we called our dogs to come with us and headed toward the field and the sheep. As we neared the house, I was startled to see Sandy sitting out on the deck. I could feel his eyes drilling into me, but I resisted the urge to look at him.

As we moved past, Sandy called out softly, his voice mockingly sweet, "Whispers are lies."

Jason, Matthew, and I all knew that line well. Anytime Sandy couldn't hear our conversation, that's what he'd say.

My skin tingled and my face burned. It took a huge effort to keep moving past him. I felt like a fly in a spider's web. A bug on a pin. But without saying a word, Matthew and I continued past the house and out onto the field.

"Why don't we let Lady go out around the sheep and bring them in?" I said to Mat. "That way she'll get to work a little bit. She doesn't realize she's too old to work like she did when she was in her prime. She'd work till she drops dead if I let her."

I tied Zeke to the fence using a short chain with a snap on each end. With Zeke secured, I gave Lady the command, "Come by," meaning she should head out to the left and make a loop around the sheep. They were a good half kilometre away. She took off instantly, staying well wide so she wouldn't spook the sheep before she got to the opposite side of them. She made a perfect outrun. That was due partly to her border collie instinct, and partly to the training my friends Dennis and Jean Gellings had done with her after I became paralyzed.

When she reached the far side of the flock, Lady walked in toward them. The sheep headed straight for me, with Lady following behind. When they got to where I was sitting, I said quietly, "Lie down, Lady." She stopped where she was, taking the pressure off the sheep. They remained near me in a little clump.

In the spring of 1995, my cousin Emilie had shown up at the farm with a cute border collie puppy. "Here," she said. "Now that you and Sandy have quit horse racing full time, and you're not on the road anymore, you'll have time to learn how to train a stock dog."

I had watched Emilie training her stock dogs on their farm the year before and had commented to her that if I ever quit horse racing, I'd love to try working with dogs myself. It surprised me when she showed up with the puppy, but I was thrilled. I decided on the name Lady for my new little friend.

On Emilie's recommendation, I purchased a book called *The Farmer's Dog* by John Holmes and set about training Lady. As the book instructed, once Lady was about eight months old I borrowed some ducks from a neighbour for Lady to work. I made a round wire pen for the ducks so that Lady could go around and around them. I taught her to go in the direction I indicated and to lie down on command. After a few weeks, I took the ducks out of the pen and worked Lady on them all over the farm. Once she grew bored with the ducks, I bought four cull ewes from the auction mart to work her on. The ewes were horrible, cranky old girls. The only way I could control them was to catch them one by one, tie them to the fence, then tie them all together and drag them in a group out to the field. There I anchored them with a stake in the ground so Lady could go around them. If the ewes were left loose, they attacked my young dog or intimidated her.

In May 1996, I had entered Lady in the novice event at a stock dog trial at Dennis and Jean Gellings' farm in Bear Canyon, a two-and-a-half-hour drive from our farm. I was feeling thrilled with Lady's performance as she circled the sheep and brought them toward me. Then it all went south. She chased the sheep through the fence and out the other side of the barnyard, with me running behind. I finally caught her when the sheep ran into a small corral. "I'm so sorry," I said when I got back to where everyone was waiting. "I doubt you'll ever let me come back here again."

Dennis and Jean laughed. "That happens to everyone," they assured me. "It's not as easy as it looks, but hang in there. You'll get her trained if you keep at it."

Two months later, I had the spill that left me paralyzed.

Lady was left to fend for herself. Other than come into the yard to eat her dog food, she stayed in the corrals with the sheep. With me in the hospital for more than three months, and unable to care for her even when I did get home, she was abandoned.

I decided one day as I sat at the patio window that I would give Lady away. I watched her slinking toward the house, as Sandy screamed at her from the corral, "Lady! You get back here!"

Time and time again, Sandy had dragged her out and tried to make her round up the cows for him. Lady kept trying, but she could never please him, and she invariably got cursed and yelled at until she hid away somewhere. That afternoon, she simply refused to go with him. I knew she was done.

I put the word out that if anyone wanted Lady, they could have her. Jean Gellings called to say, "Why don't you bring her over? If she's not completely ruined by now, we'll work with her and get her trained."

Sandy and I headed to the Gellings' farm in Bear Canyon with Lady in tow. As I unloaded from the van on my lift, Lady went streaking past me. My lungs had been left at half capacity after my accident, and Lady ignored my shouted command for her to come back. Dennis shook his head. "Yeah, I thought she might be wrecked. I'm sorry, Holly. All we can do is hope she comes back, or that we find her if she's run off somewhere."

We stood around feeling dejected about the waste of such a promising young dog. But suddenly Dennis said, "Listen."

We looked to the north, and there came Lady, herding a flock of sheep in front of her. She delivered them to Dennis and gave him a look that could only have meant, "What do you want me to do next, boss?"

Dennis and Jean kept Lady and worked with her all summer. In the fall, my friend and fellow stock dog trainer, Ruth Finch, hosted a stock dog clinic at their ranch just south of Grande Prairie, with Dennis as instructor. He brought Lady with him, and he coached Lady and me together. Always the jokester, Dennis was fond of teasing me. "Your handicap isn't your body," he'd say, "it's between your ears. You have to learn to control Lady with your mind."

I did learn to control Lady, and I started competing across the province in novice and pro-novice stock dog trials. As I improved, I got some new puppies to train. One of them was Tank. Mat hadn't been interested in the dog training until he had to pick me up off the ground one day. I'd been in the corral with a dozen sheep and Tank in training. The objective was for Tank to circle the sheep and hold them to me. Tank was an aggressive pup. He did his job too well, and he ended up pushing the sheep right on top of me, knocking me off my four-wheel scooter. I yelled at Tank to stop, which only made him more aggressive and excited. Mat was working in the shop nearby, and he stuck his head out to see what the commotion was. He ran over, caught Tank, and rescued me. I talked him into helping me train Tank after that, and he fell in love with both the sport and the dog.

It's impossible to dwell on anything else while you're working a stock dog. It takes your full concentration, so it's a great way to get your mind off your troubles. That afternoon Mat and I took turns working our dogs, him with Tank and me with Zeke and Lady. We worked on getting them to obey commands, and to stop with one short whistle blast. We had worked them in the Highland Games stock dog trial in Grande Prairie a few days before, and they hadn't done very well. We needed to squeeze in every bit of practice we could before going to any more trials.

We were still working the dogs when my friend Laurie Wedler showed up. She parked her truck near the house, unloaded her border collie, Splash, and headed out to join us. She worked Splash on the sheep for twenty minutes or so, with Mat and me giving the odd bit of advice from the sidelines. When she was done, we gave all the dogs a drink, and the three of us talked about the two new rams I had just purchased.

"Do you think Sandy will go get them?" Laurie asked.

"Oh, I'm sure he will," I said. "He loves road trips."

"Great. I'll help you get the truck ready," Laurie said.

Laurie was fit and solid, and she thought nothing of wrestling a two-hundred-pound sheep to the ground to shear or doctor it. I'd met her about five years before on the dog trial circuit, and she'd become a regular at working stock dogs with Mat and me.

Sandy had worked hard to impress Laurie, as he did with nearly everyone at first, wooing and courting her with all the charm he could muster. I'd seen it hundreds of times by then, and I had originally been enticed by it myself. Sandy could make his target feel like the most special person in the world. He had started to relax his guard around Laurie though, and I could see her beginning to realize Sandy wasn't the person he pretended he was. When I commented to her one day that I was impressed with how she remained neutral with Sandy, indicating neither pleasure nor displeasure, she replied, "When I went to college to learn to be a veterinary technician, part of my instruction was on how to recognize and deal with difficult people. I can see he's one of those guys you have to be very careful around. I just try to steer clear of him if I can."

We were still chatting about the rams when we heard Sandy's quad start up. It was either that or the tractor; he never walked anywhere. He came roaring up to us before we could scatter, sitting sidesaddle on his quad like he always did when he was planning to do battle.

The quad halted with a lurch, screeching as Sandy clamped the handbrake tight. He jumped off before it came to a complete stop. His stomach thrust out ahead of him, straining to escape his plaid western shirt. One pearl snap-button was undone, and his belly button protruded from the gap. The button above his zipper fly was open. He must have forgotten to do it up when he rose from his recliner, where he always loosened his pants to release the pressure on his mid-section. I winced as a waft of his rank body odour hit me.

"What are you guys talking about?" he growled, glaring at me. A dribble of chewing tobacco had escaped the corner of his mouth and was trickling down his chin.

Mat and Laurie subtly backed away. Their dogs slunk over beside them, eyeing Sandy warily. Zeke and Lady bumped against the back of my wheelchair. I knew they were hiding from Sandy. The threat of violence hung in the air.

I piped up nervously, not sure what Sandy was going to do. "We were just saying it would sure be nice if you'd go pick up those rams I bought."

His scowl turned to a smirk. A silly little-girl giggle escaped him, soon becoming a loud guffaw. "So you need a real truck driver, huh? Can't do anything without me, can you? *Hyuk yuk yuk.*"

"Sure," I said, my scalp prickling with distaste, disgusted with myself for grovelling. My stomach turned as I watched him swagger back to his quad.

CHAPTER 3

IN 1979, THE summer Sandy Crichton and I met, I was a successful jockey on the Alberta Community Racing Circuit. I'd always been a free spirit, living on the edge and taking risks in everything I did. On a horse's back, I felt invincible.

My brother Gordie had died the fall before, which affected me deeply. On September 5, 1978, sixteen days before his twenty-second birthday, he was a passenger in a de Havilland Beaver airplane, flying in to a job he was finishing for the British Columbia Parks Branch. With draft horses to skid the logs, his team of three young men was building a log tourist cabin using only chainsaws and hand tools.

Gordie had spent the September long weekend with me at the ranch I was working on, near Kamloops. We'd talked about our hopes and dreams while he helped me clean stalls and stack hay bales. His plan, once his BC Parks contract was complete, was to solo portage the popular Bowran Lakes Chain. He had his canoe and supplies all ready to go. Gordie left the ranch on Tuesday morning and headed to the Kamloops airport. Later that day, the charter plane he and his crew were on crashed en route. Everyone on board was killed instantly. I was twenty years old, and for the first time in my life, I had to deal with a tragedy.

Gordie had been the "golden boy" in our family. He was the perfect package, headed for great things in life. And unlike my brother Danny and me, Gordie had been cautious. "Safety first" was his mantra. I'd always been a daredevil, but after his death I threw caution to the wind and began to push everything I did to the limit. I abandoned my parents to their grief, setting off on my own quest. I left the rodeo and show-horse world I'd been living in and headed for the racetrack.

⪶

When I was young, I had lived in a number of places throughout BC and Alberta. We travelled with my dad as he followed construction jobs. Some of the houses the five of us lived in had plumbing, some didn't; some were in town, some weren't. There was never money for luxuries, but we were always together, and we never went hungry. There was often a friend or neighbour at the supper table. My mom loved to have people over and to have a reason to use her china and silverware.

My dad's uncle, Erling Nergaard, had a small sawmill near Tête Jaune, BC, and he also owned a forty-acre parcel of land close to the town of Valemount. When I was eight, Dad went to work for Erling, and we moved onto his property. We lived in Erling's "big house," which had about seven hundred square feet of space. Erling moved into a tiny cabin that he and Dad quickly constructed, and Mom's mother joined us too, taking up residence in another tiny house made with planks from Erling's mill.

Uncle Erling's forty acres was fenced, and the Mortensons, who owned the grocery store in town, boarded two horses there. I spent all of my time out in the field sitting bareback on them, letting them take me wherever they went. That's where my love affair with horses began.

Dad had worked a bit with horses as a young man doing jobs on farms near Shell Lake, Saskatchewan, where he was born and raised. His father was a carpenter though, not a farmer, so horses hadn't been a big part of his life. Mom's father trapped and hunted, and she got very skilled with horses as a kid, but she wasn't around them after she grew up. My greatest desire was to someday have a horse of my own. I could talk my mom into anything, and my parents agreed to buy me a horse named Merrylegs, a two-year-old filly, for my eleventh birthday.

By this time, Dad was working as a catskinner on the construction of the Trans-Canada Highway. His boss, Elmer Roth, had a wooden leg, which fascinated me. Elmer had also spent his youth catching and training wild horses. Everybody knew he was magical with a horse. One afternoon during a visit to our place,

Elmer told me, "I can teach you to train Merrylegs, but you'll have to do all the riding yourself. I can't get on a horse anymore because of this darn leg."

"What happened to your real leg?" I asked, my curiosity overcoming my shyness.

"I got run over by a loaded coal wagon, and my leg was crushed. It couldn't be saved."

Elmer and I started working with Merrylegs together. I was a quick study, and I loved what I was learning. One day when he arrived after work, Elmer said, "Today's the day you get to ride without me holding you on a lunge line. It's time to try riding on your own."

"No problem," I said, confident I could do it.

It didn't take me long to get Merrylegs caught and her bridle on. There wasn't a saddle to worry about. My parents had splurged a hundred dollars on getting me the filly. There was no chance of me getting a saddle anytime soon.

The first few minutes were calm. Merrylegs followed the familiar routine of going in circles around Elmer. Then, not having a clue what would happen once she realized she was free, I steered her away, toward the open gate.

"Don't go out that gate!" Elmer shouted.

I yanked the reins and squeezed with my legs, sending Merrylegs, in a panic, straight through the open gate and into unknown territory. We barrelled through Mom's garden, past Uncle Erling's house, past my grandmother's house, under the spruce tree and down the trail past our house. Merrylegs headed south, running through our bachelor neighbour Frankie Plant's yard and then down the old road toward town.

Through my watering eyes, I caught a glimpse of Mom and Dad's grey '58 Chevy racing down the new gravel road that ran parallel to the one I was on. My hands full of mane were all that kept me on Merrylegs' sweaty back as she streaked along, racing full bore. Somehow I managed to stay on when she jumped the train tracks about a mile from town, and eventually she started to tire. As we approached the bridge over Swift Creek, she slowed to a lope. Having never crossed a bridge before, Merrylegs slammed on the brakes when she saw it, spinning me over her head and onto the gravel road.

Dad skidded the car to a stop. Elmer stumbled out of the back seat and limped off to catch the horse while Mom and Dad rushed over to me.

"That goddamn horse," Mom yelled. "I'll kill it!" I'd never heard her swear before, and she scared me worse than the horse had.

I cried for a while, then picked myself up when I realized I wasn't hurt. Elmer suggested we could lead Merrylegs home from the car window. "It wasn't the horse's fault," he said, earning himself a scorching glare from Mom. Everyone looked at me expectantly, waiting for me to get in the car. I was having none of that. They might lead my horse from the car window, but it would be with me on her back.

As we crept along toward home, euphoria took hold. I might have been a pudgy little eleven-year-old whose brothers called her Hobby Gob. I couldn't run fast, jump high, or answer math questions. But I knew I could ride a racing horse.

The years we spent living near Valemount were wonderful, but they didn't last. My brother Danny had to go away for high school, since the school in Valemount only went up to grade nine. He lived in school dorms in both McBride and Prince George, where he fell in with a bad crowd and was soon using and selling drugs. Mom was convinced that it would mean nothing but trouble for Gordie and me to go the same route. The clincher came when I was thirteen. My parents got a phone call from the school, where an evening sock hop was being held. "Come and get Holly," the teachers told them. "She's drunk. Throwing up in the bathroom."

"We're moving to Kamloops," Mom said the next morning.

My main concern was my horse. What would happen to her? I begged and promised I would never take a wrong step again if my parents would only find a way to bring Merrylegs along. As luck would have it, by this time Elmer Roth lived on the north side of Kamloops on a small acreage. He agreed Merrylegs could be boarded there.

Mom and Dad got a contract cleaning the agricultural research station in Kamloops, and Gordie and I were enrolled in school. Elmer lived on the far side of the city from us, so I could only ride my horse about once a week. I took my little black chihuahua cross dog, Chiquita, to obedience classes at Cariboo College, where my brother Danny was taking a hotel/motel management course. Even so, I had far too much energy and free time on my hands. I found trouble, or it found me. I started smoking pot and skipping school. Once again, Mom told us we were moving.

This time my parents decided to go to the Douglas Lake Ranch, which was in the middle of nowhere. Mom had been married before she met my dad, and she had a daughter named Bobbi from that marriage. Bobbi was sixteen years older than me; she was married and gone from home by the time I was two. Bobbi lived in Kamloops with her husband and three sons, and Gordie begged to be allowed to stay with her to finish high school there. That meant it was just my parents and me at Douglas Lake. I hadn't wanted to go, but the place turned out to suit me to a T. I spent my free time either riding the range with one cowboy crew or another, or practising for high school rodeo events. In each rodeo, I'd enter up to seven events: barrel racing, pole bending, goat tying, steer riding, cutting, breakaway roping, and team roping. The Douglas Lake Ranch was a legendary place, the largest working ranch in Canada, and many people came there to ride or to fly-fish. My parents couldn't have found a better place for me.

⁂

The day after I graduated from high school in June 1976, I headed off to work for a veterinarian I had met at the ranch. From there, I worked for three different cutting-horse trainers. After Gordie died, I started racing.

My devil-may-care attitude at the track, combined with the fact that I was a natural rider and horses loved to run for me, set me up to win a lot of races. It also set me up for resentment from some of my fellow riders. I had no regard for my own safety, and my aggressive but uneducated riding created dangerous situations. Life was one big party for me.

Sandy Crichton was running horses on the Alberta B circuit where I rode. The first time I noticed him, he was yelling at someone for putting a horse in the wrong stall. My first impression was negative, but I never saw that side of Sandy again as the summer progressed. He was charming and attractive and always went out of his way to treat me well. I forgot about my initial bad vibes.

At the racetrack, riders are hired by trainers to either exercise or race their horses. I rode for nearly every trainer on the circuit over the summer. Sandy hired me to ride his horses, and we started spending time together, chatting in the shed row or having breakfast together at a café after morning training. He ate up the stories I told him of my teenage years at the Douglas Lake Cattle Company, and my subsequent travels with the rodeo crowd. My action-packed tales were filled with famous names and legendary places.

Sandy insisted on hearing these stories over and over, seemingly fascinated by every detail. I told him about my pampered early years as the youngest child of parents who doted on me. Then, when I was fourteen, my sneaking out at night and roaming the streets of Kamloops. I hadn't taken to school much, but I got well educated in the ways of street thugs, using and selling drugs with the people I met. I told Sandy about the nights I'd later spent in jail for being drunk and disorderly and about the beating I'd taken from a hooker on the streets of Edmonton when I asked her out of curiosity, "How much money do you make on an average night?" I told him everything about myself.

The charge I got from being obsessively pursued by an older, successful racehorse trainer went to my head. Sandy's attention convinced me that I was a superstar, somebody special. The more arrogant and cocky I got, the better I did on the racetrack. The better I did on the racetrack, the cockier and more arrogant I got.

After that summer of racing in Alberta, I learned Sandy was planning to take his horses to Regina, Saskatchewan, for the fall meet. A couple I'd been riding for were going down as well. I was glad to have the opportunity to go to a higher-calibre racetrack, especially with the guaranteed foot-in-the-door of having horses I knew would run well for me.

I started off with a bang in Regina, making headlines for winning my first race, then being disqualified for careless riding. The stewards, or judges, in Regina were a lot tougher on me than they had been in Alberta. They didn't find my antics amusing in the least. After a few suspensions and fines, I learned to "pick my head up" as it's called at the track. Still I always pushed the envelope and rode tight.

I hadn't been in Regina long before a few riders in the jocks room started to harass me, hoping to put me in my place through threats and intimidation. In those days there weren't rules regarding workplace bullying. It was every man for himself, and I was pushing my way into a male-dominated sport. Looking back, I don't blame other riders for being angry with me. Riding came easily to me, and I had a lot of success, winning over a hundred races that season without paying my dues or struggling to rise up the ladder. I lived life from one joy ride to the next.

Some of the altercations with my detractors were public, boiling over into shouting and shoving matches as we walked back to the jocks room after a race. Sandy Crichton was a powerful man, and he took it upon himself to back me up. He became my enforcer, threatening to break arms if my harassers didn't back off. Suddenly, it wasn't just me the other jockeys were dealing with. Once I realized I didn't have to worry about them, my attitude knew no bounds.

My relationship with Sandy sparked into romance as fall progressed. With his rugged features and confident stance, intense blue eyes, and arms like fence posts, he made me feel safe and protected in the often-volatile life I was leading. I was also attracted to his raw power and ambition. Sandy was the racehorse trainer, and I was the hot-shot rider. We made a successful team, winning races and having fun. Sandy treated me like a goddess, constantly feeding my ego with compliments. I was twenty-one years old to his forty-two, but I never felt as if there was an imbalance of power. Two of my best-loved mentors from the Douglas Lake Cattle Company, Stan and Diane Murphy, had a large age gap between them and they were great together. Besides, despite the intense chemistry between Sandy and me, I had no thoughts of anything long-term. He was there, I was there, and we were both single. The last thing I wanted was to be tied down. I was having far too much fun in my life to want to change anything.

Sandy was obsessed with knowing everything about my past romances. The conversations usually started with him teasing me.

"I'll bet you had all the guys trying to get into your pants," he'd say. I was embarrassed by his words, but I took them as a compliment. He pried further, pushing for details. I'd been a teenager during the '70s, and being sexually active was normal where I lived. I had no feelings of shame or any need to hide my past. Although I was a bit weirded out by Sandy's intense interest in my history, it made me feel attractive and powerful to have an older man that I saw as accomplished and intelligent be so fixated on me. He told me of the limited number of women he had been sexually active with, saying he had always been shy around women. He was so emotional and genuine that I never had a moment's doubt about his sincerity. Earlier in the summer he'd had a woman around my age with him at a few race meets. He told me she'd been his girlfriend for a year or so, but they were no longer together. The racetrack was a world of its own, and I was a shining star in the spotlight. I had no interest in Sandy's outside life, and no reason to care about his past.

When the Regina race meet was finished in November, I headed to my parents' place for winter. They'd moved back to Valemount, and I had plans to break horses there until spring. I had just gotten settled when Sandy phoned to ask if I'd break a horse for him as well. I agreed, and he hauled it to Valemount for me. After I was finished breaking his horse, he came back to pick it up. While he was there, he asked if I would come to his farm in the spring to train racehorses, then go on to the track with him. Since our previous year had been so good, I agreed to the plan.

CHAPTER 4

I PACKED UP my tack in early 1980 and headed to Sandy's farm. I was surprised at the lack of facilities when I arrived at his isolated yard site, over three kilometres down a rutted, dead-end road, surrounded by woods and about forty kilometres from Grande Prairie. "Oh well," I told myself. "It will be an adventure training racehorses out in the wilderness." Sandy and I carried on where we'd left off the fall before, working seamlessly together as a team, each with the same work ethic and goals.

I learned that he owned two, mostly treed, quarter sections at his homesite, and two cleared quarters six kilometres southwest. In the years to come, we would add another quarter section to each site, making them 480 acres each. He was still married to a woman named Mary, he revealed, but she had filed for divorce and he had only to sign the papers to finalize it. They had no children. That part of his life sounded uncomplicated, and it didn't cause me any discomfort. All I cared about was horse racing, and he seemed to have the same passion. Before long, I fell madly in love with him. I thought we were perfectly suited to each other.

I didn't know anyone in the area, and training horses filled my time. So, other than going to town on occasion for supplies, I stayed out at the farm. Without realizing it over the spring and summer, I became cut off from all my friends. Before we loaded up the horses and headed for the racetrack in Saskatchewan, I'd given Sandy the twelve thousand dollars I had saved the summer before to have a new training barn built at his farm. When we got back after a very successful season, a lovely twelve-stall barn and indoor training area was waiting for us. I was committed to the relationship by then, and we decided to start a family. Sandy told me he had always wanted children, and I thought, *why not?*

in my usual impulsive way. By late November, I was pregnant. Everything was fairytale wonderful as my pregnancy advanced.

About a month before the baby was due, a young relative of mine came to stay at the farm with us. Tracy was just twelve years old, from a troubled home, and I wanted to give her a chance at having a normal, happy summer. I was delighted that Sandy was in favour of her visit, and he seemed to like her once she arrived.

I couldn't ride with Tracy because of my advanced pregnancy, but I coached her and helped her from the ground as much as I could. When she wasn't riding, she had the entire farm to ramble around on. I was in full support when Sandy told me she wanted to ride a horse of her own with him in the local parade. But our conversation took an unexpected turn when I warned him he should be careful in his dealings with Tracy, since the story in the family was that she'd started some trouble by accusing her stepfather of being inappropriate with her. "The last thing you need is to be accused of messing with a little girl," I said.

Sandy's reply shocked me. "She has to learn sometime. It may as well be from someone she trusts."

Was he saying it was okay if Tracy's stepfather had molested her? I came unglued, telling him in no uncertain terms what I thought of pedophiles. "If he did mess with her, the sicko should go to prison!" I said heatedly.

Sandy got defensive, claiming I'd heard him wrong. He accused me of having a guilty conscience myself by leaping instantly to thinking dirty thoughts the way I just had. He made me feel sorry for jumping on him, and I apologized, shaken. How could I for one minute have thought he would condone Tracy's stepfather being a pervert? I must have misheard him.

Tracy did get to ride in the parade, but that same day she decided abruptly to leave the farm, a week earlier than planned. I was sad to see her go, but she was determined not to stay any longer. I thought she might have been homesick.

Sandy became noticeably irritable after Tracy left. He was surly with me and found fault with everything I did. I was disturbed by his bad mood. Life had seemed perfect up until then. About a week later he attacked me physically for the first time.

It was a beautiful day in mid-August, the sun high to the south in a blue, blue sky. Sandy and I strolled out after lunch to begin the job we'd planned of building a fence around the house. His foul mood seemed to be gone, and I was relieved that things were back to normal.

Sandy's winter occupation was contract logging, and he kept two John Deere log skidders parked at the farm. The plan was for me to drive one of them, pushing the new fence posts into the ground with the dozer blade at the front of the skidder.

With Sandy bracing me from behind, I stretched my leg to reach the skidder's bottom step. We laughed about how clumsy I was with my big belly in the way. Sandy was so capable and competent. As I settled myself onto the driver's seat, I felt there was no way on earth I could be happier.

One by one, Sandy set the sharpened posts in their proper spot. I manoeuvred the dozer blade above them. Everything had to be perfectly straight, or the post would go in crooked. Whenever that happened, Sandy had to wrap a chain around the post and attach the chain to the dozer blade. I would raise the blade, wrenching the post back out of the ground, then get lined up again, and re-sink it.

I'm just a touch over five feet tall. With my big belly in the way, my legs and arms simply weren't long enough to reach all the controls, and I had trouble reaching across to work the hydraulics that lowered the blade. The job was slow going, but we were gaining ground. In spite of the difficulty I was having, I was delighted with our progress. Then, suddenly, everything changed.

One minute Sandy was in a jovial mood, making jokes about my lack of talent as a skidder operator. Then, as if a switch had been flipped, he started yelling. "You have to be a fucking cunt, don't you? If there's one thing I can't stand, it's a sneak and a liar!"

I didn't know what was wrong, and I was terrified. I froze, afraid to move and possibly make something worse. Maybe I'd driven the skidder into a bad spot, or run over something.

By now Sandy was really screaming. "You think you're so much better than me!"

He continued to rave. The more he ranted, the less sense he made. Finally I got angry at his senseless tirade. I slammed the skidder into park and clambered off. "What's wrong with you?" I shouted. "You can talk to me in a civil way, or you won't be getting any help from me at all!"

In an instant he had me by the hair, shaking me like a rag doll and flinging me to the ground.

"What did you say to me?" he bellowed as he towered over me.

"Get the hell away from me," I yelled. "Are you crazy or something?"

Sandy grabbed me by the throat, digging his fingers in, then switched his grip back to my hair and slammed my head into the ground. "Don't you *ever, ever* call me crazy!"

As he glared down at me, the intense blue eyes I'd been drawn to like a moth to a flame cut through me, radiating pure, unmasked hatred. My stomach churned.

I'd never seen anyone go into this kind of rage. But I'd never backed down from anyone before, either. It was inconceivable to me that anyone, much less the man I loved, would feel he had the right to hit me and choke me and call me filthy names. I was crying as I yelled at Sandy, "I won't put up with this shit. Who the hell do you think you are?"

He dragged me over to the skidder by the hair and flung me at the steps. "I'll show you who I am. You get the fuck up there. We're not done here!"

We tussled some more. I tried to stand my ground and defy him, but in the end, after more choking and slapping, I got up on the skidder, and we finished pushing the posts into the ground. As we worked Sandy continued to rail on about how I thought I was better than he was. "You don't have your daddy to look after you anymore," he spewed. "You're mine now! You'll do what I say!" His open hatred and disgust left me bewildered and heartbroken.

After we'd finished installing the posts, I lay on our bed and sobbed. When I heard Sandy enter the house, I assumed he'd come to apologize and to explain what had caused such extreme behaviour. He did come into the bedroom, but rather than apologizing, he blurted, "Are you just gonna lie there blubbering all day? We've got more work to do if you want that fence made. Get your ass out there and help me!"

I was dreadfully ashamed, and scared stiff as well. I got up and went back outside.

That night when Sandy came to bed, he acted as if nothing had happened. I was still stunned by his actions, but I wasn't as emotional as I'd been earlier. Why had he blown up so badly, I asked him. What could possibly have caused him to be so angry?

"You're doing this to me. If there's one thing I can't stand it's a sneak and a liar. I put you on a pedestal and look what you're doing to me!" he replied angrily.

"What are you talking about? What have I done to you?"

"You know!" he shouted. "You know!"

"What the hell are you talking about?"

"If you think you're gonna control me, think again. No woman is gonna control me!"

He was making no sense at all. "You'll never have to worry about that from me," I yelled. I jumped out of bed and began pulling my clothes from the dresser drawers, stuffing them into my suitcase.

Sandy started sobbing frantically. "Where do you think you're going?" he yelled. "You get back in this bed! You're not leaving here!"

When he jumped up and came at me, I ran out into the dining room. He chased me down and cornered me behind the table. He grabbed me by the throat, choking and shaking me and banging my head against the wall. I cried out for him to stop, but that only made him worse. He kept screaming as he thumped my head against the wall, "Shut up, you fucking cunt. You think you can control me just because you have a cute little ass. I'll show you who's in control here."

Finally, I did shut up. I quit struggling and went limp. For the first time in my life, I knew real fear.

Sandy gathered me in his arms in the unlit dining room. Through sobs, he told me he loved me so much he couldn't stand the thought of losing me. He would kill me and then himself if I left him, he said. And it would only take one match to send my parents' place up in flames if I thought I could hide there. "I know everything about you," he hissed. "There's nowhere you can go that I won't find you."

I couldn't understand how my life had gone from blissfully happy to miserable and terrifying in the blink of an eye. I was disoriented, not really sure what was happening, aware only that I'd gotten myself into something that was way over my head. All I knew was that my initial perception of Sandy was proving to be horribly wrong.

The day after that first beating, feeling utterly devoid of hope, I poured myself a drink. I'd taken only a few sips from it, though, when I realized what I was doing. By drinking, I'd be putting my baby at risk, devastating my parents, and betraying my own moral code. Whatever his reasons for wanting to damage me, if I drowned myself in booze, Sandy would succeed in his mission. I could never let my guard down with him again, I decided, and alcohol would make me even more vulnerable. I made a clear, conscious choice then and there. I was in a horrible situation I could see no escape from, but I would not give up on who I was inside. Sandy could never control my mind.

CHAPTER 5

TWO WEEKS LATER, on August 25, my water broke as I was getting ready for bed. I asked Sandy to take me to the hospital, a forty-five-minute drive away. He was surly for the entire trip, refusing to look at me or to say a word. He dropped me off in the dark hospital parking area. I expected him to park the pickup and then join me. But he drove away, never looking back. Clutching the overnight bag I'd packed with spare clothes and toiletries, I watched until he was out of sight, then made the lonely trek up the stairs and into the hospital.

After twenty hours of labour, my doctor decided to perform a Caesarean delivery. The hospital staff hadn't been able to reach Sandy to tell him I was having trouble. By then I was so played out I didn't care. Sandy walked in just as they were wheeling me into surgery.

I was overcome with relief when I saw my baby the next morning. Sandy was thrilled with Jason and, after his birth, he went back to being the charming man I'd fallen in love with. I wondered if I'd imagined the intensity of his fury. Maybe I'd overreacted. Maybe it hadn't really been that big a deal. Everyone else seemed to think highly of Sandy. He was the best neighbour in the world. He would drop everything, at any time of the day or night, to rush to help someone in need. Frozen water lines? A cow calving at three in the morning? Tractor broken down? No problem. Sandy was the man to call.

Sandy was proud to have a son. As long as he didn't have to change Jason's diaper, he liked nothing better than to take the baby out and show him off. He'd rock Jason's cradle with his toe, or carry him around when he fussed.

Occasionally I'd see signs of aggression in Sandy, but not aimed at me. He complained bitterly about his mother, who had died before I met him, telling me she had never been affectionate with him like my mother was with me. He'd get agitated when talking about his ex-wife, Mary. She had been unreliable, he said, always feeling sorry for herself and running off; he'd have to go find her and bring her home again. I assured him I would never let him down like his mother and Mary had. Shortly after he signed the divorce papers, we learned that Mary had been killed in a motor-vehicle collision.

I had no understanding of domestic violence. My father was a kind and gentle man. I never saw him deliberately harm anyone or anything. All the men I'd known were honourable, respectful of their wives and children. So despite my alarm at Sandy's actions, I still believed he was a good man. I couldn't conceive of anything else. I loved him for the admirable qualities he had, and I decided that his one slip into violence should be forgiven and forgotten. We decided to have another child, and Matthew was born on January 14, 1983.

Motherly instincts I couldn't have imagined kicked in when my babies were born. Jason and Matthew became without question the most important thing in my life. I would have stepped in front of a speeding train for them. Sandy knew that, and I thought he supported my feelings. But by the time Jason was around three years old, Sandy was leveraging my love for my sons.

It started with small insults and slaps, always justified by Sandy with something I'd done to deserve them. At first I fought back. But he would escalate the force until I gave in and apologized to him, and I learned not to argue or disagree. There were more times early on where I told him I'd leave if he didn't change his ways. But he convinced me I had no options. If I wanted the boys to have a mother and not be raised in a foster home, he threatened, I'd better toe the line. He reminded me he knew everything about my past and would track me down no matter where I went.

I could not put my sons in the position of being orphans or having their mother killed, so I resigned myself to my fate. I threw myself into controlling what I could control, which was my ability to be a good mother and a good worker. I thought I could extend my protective shell to cover Jason and Matthew and tried my best to do so as time passed.

Sandy would never show his true colours in public. It was hypocritical living in a situation where we looked like a happy family, but being a hypocrite was preferable to being a punching bag. The years as the boys grew up were peppered with bizarre, disturbing episodes where Sandy would go off the rails, but though I could never understand his behaviour, I learned to live with it. The saving grace was that when our sons were young children, Sandy was away for most of the year, either logging or racing horses. We got to live a normal happy life when he wasn't around.

Usually, no matter what he'd been like that day, when we went to bed at night Sandy would be loving. I treasured the closeness of his nighttime persona until I realized that if he was particularly kind and loving at night, he'd be proportionally more violent the next day.

There was one horrible episode I wouldn't understand until years later. We were cuddling in bed one night when Sandy said to me, "You must have been such a cute little girl. That makes me so horny."

"Whoa. What a twisted thing to say," I said.

Jerking away from me harshly, he snarled, "You always have to twist my words and try to make something dirty of me."

"Settle down. Why are you so sensitive?"

Glaring at me, he said, "You think you're so much better than me. I was trying to give you a compliment, and you have to screw it all up. You must have a guilty conscience or something." He rolled over, turning his back to me.

I felt bad for hurting his feelings.

The boys and I sensed that Sandy was in a bad mood the next morning and breakfast was a silent affair. When he got up from the table I asked what his plans were for the day. All I got in reply was a grunt. He got in his truck and drove off, not returning until suppertime, still in a foul mood.

As we lay in bed that night, Sandy started quietly sobbing. When I put my arms around him and asked what was wrong, he cried out, "Why don't you help me? Can't you see I need help? I'm begging you to help me!"

"I can't help you unless I know what's bothering you," I said, trying to comfort him. "Please tell me what it is."

By then Sandy and I were trying to make a go of it with our horse-training business as our only income. Things were tight financially. Maybe that was his problem, and he just didn't know how to talk about it. "Would you like me to make you an appointment to talk to a doctor?" I asked him.

His agitation increased, and I finally quit talking. I lay there listening to him sob and rant, hoping he would settle down soon and go to sleep. The next night was the same, he alternated between crying and grabbing and shaking me. "I need help, can't you see that? You don't even try to understand me!"

"You're right," I repeated over and over. "I don't understand you. You have to tell me what's wrong. Maybe then I can help you."

His sobs became louder and angrier, building up until he lashed out again.

On the third night, I decided I would take a stand if he pushed me around again. I'd done nothing wrong, and I was tired of him harassing me, shaking me, and calling me names.

While Sandy was in the bathroom, I got a large wrench and slipped it under my pillow. Soon after we got into bed, he started sobbing again. "I'm begging you to help me. Can't you see I need help? Why won't you help me?"

"You have to talk to me," I said firmly. "Tell me what's wrong with you. Or I can make you an appointment with a doctor. I'll go with you if you want."

"You think I'm crazy? You think I'm crazy? Well, I'm not!"

Sandy jumped on top of me and started slamming me against the bed. "I'll show you crazy," he bellowed. "You haven't seen anything."

I reached under my pillow, got hold of the wrench, and hit him with it. He went wild, springing up and flinging me into the closet. He came at me, slapping and kicking. Finally, he backed off and left me there, with shoes and clothes scattered all around. As I cringed on the closet floor, I heard him panting. "I didn't even hurt you. If I wanted to hurt you, I could. You have no idea what I'm capable of. I never even closed my fists!"

I spent the night in the closet, covering myself as best I could with clothes that had fallen off their hangers in the fracas. As I lay there, I decided I would leave Sandy no matter what the consequences. Things couldn't get a whole lot scarier or crazier than what I was already going through.

Nothing was said the next morning as I served Sandy his usual breakfast: half a grapefruit, two slices of lightly buttered whole wheat toast, a bowl of homemade fruit salad, and two cups of black coffee. Mat was barely out of diapers and sat on his booster chair, with his brother sitting on the chair next to him. They ate their Cheerios and drank their apple juice in silence.

When Sandy left, headed for our field six kilometres away where he was seeding barley, I took a small stash of cash I had tucked away, and hid it under the floor mat of the Datsun pickup that my parents had given me when I went out on my own. I quickly packed a duffle bag with spare clothes for the boys and me, and hid it behind the seat. I left the boys in the house until I had the truck lined up and headed down the driveway. After listening for the sound of any approaching vehicles on our remote road, and hearing nothing, I ran into the house, grabbed a boy under each arm and dashed out to the Datsun.

It was a terrifying experience going down our two-and-a-half-kilometre driveway. I was petrified Sandy would somehow catch us leaving.

The only person I knew well enough to go to for help was our old neighbour, Ann Topley. Ann had lived with her husband, Em, on a farm a few miles from us, but when Em died, she'd moved into Grande Prairie. I had no idea what I was going to do. I surprised Ann by showing up at her place unannounced. She told me about the women's shelter, and went with me to show me where it was.

That afternoon, Sandy arrived at the shelter looking for me. The shelter's location was supposed to be secret, but the staff told me Sandy was outside, banging on the door and demanding to see me. I learned years later that he had gone to Ann Topley's and she'd told him where I was. Sandy was not allowed in, and after a while he finally went away. The next day, he came back. The shelter's staff advised me not to talk to him. If I did, they said, I'd have to call him on the phone or meet him somewhere away from the shelter. In those days, there was nothing really organized to help women and children who were fleeing domestic violence. The shelter could only feed us and give us a bed for a few days. I was afraid of what would happen when our time there was up.

If I left Sandy, I knew I'd be forfeiting my financial investment in the farm, which was all of my life savings. I'd have to start all over again, on the run and hiding with two small children. The devil I knew seemed less daunting than the devil I didn't. I talked to Sandy on the phone a number of times, and he told me he was sorry for what had happened. I heard what I wanted to hear, taking his words as acknowledgement that he understood he had done wrong.

The shelter was a sad and lonely place. The boys hated it, and so did I. Although it was meant to keep women safe by locking out the men who were hunting them, it was like being in a prison. Jason and Matthew missed their home, their pets, and their freedom. I did too. I agreed to meet with Sandy, leaving the boys back at the shelter. He said all the right things. He agreed to go to counselling, and he promised never to lay a hand on me in anger again. He convinced me that he loved and needed me. I picked up the boys from the shelter, and we all drove back to the farm.

The next day, we drove to Grande Prairie and dropped the boys off with Ann Topley. Sandy and I went to a counselling session the staff at the shelter had arranged. The counsellor recommended that Sandy take an anger management course through the John Howard Society. When we left, Sandy was angry with the counsellor, and with me, saying I had poisoned the man against him. He did go to one anger management meeting in the weeks that followed; at least he told me he had. It was a stupid waste of time, he said, and he wasn't going to any more of them. "I don't need some fruitcake asshole telling me what to do," he protested. "I just need you to stop pissing me off."

I was disappointed, but I was happy to be home, and Sandy wasn't acting crazy anymore. We carried on with our lives and forgot about the counselling. Sandy never told me what had happened to set off the last episode or why he'd been so distraught, crying, and begging me to help him. I hoped he'd sorted out whatever was bothering him, and I didn't want to provoke him by mentioning it again. Although I knew deep down by now that he was unstable, it was easier to believe that I was the problem, because that was something I could work with. I could pay attention and make myself into a better person.

CHAPTER 6

I HAD STARTED back at breaking and exercising horses five months after Matthew's birth in 1983. But riding racehorses can be a dangerous business, and now that I was a mother, I was riding scared. If I got hurt, I worried, who would look after the boys?

I rode our horses because someone had to, and I was the only one who could. Sandy was too big to exercise the race-horses. He had no desire to break them, either, so the job fell to me. But I wasn't riding with confidence, and any experienced rider will tell you that's not smart. I had decided I wouldn't take any more chances than necessary. I would be cautious instead.

By the spring of 1986, Jason was nearly five, and Matti was three-and-a-half. While Sandy and I worked in the barn, the boys stayed safe in the box stall we had fixed up for them to play in, along with Jay's little blue heeler dog, Gyp, and Matti's basset hound cross, Pal. With their stall door closed and latched, there was no danger of the boys getting trampled by a loose horse or stumbling into an occupied stall. I always listened for them though, and I checked on them after every horse I exercised.

Our training track was a lumpy trail we'd made by dragging a disk through hard clay soil on a little meadow south of the barn. The track was unfenced. On the same meadow, a band of brood mares and foals ranged free. They often hung around on the infield of the little track, so I kept an eye on the mares at all times. If I got too near their babies when I galloped past, they'd charge at the horse I was on, causing it to duck or bolt.

When you work a horse, you are making it run almost full out. A thoroughbred racehorse can reach speeds of forty miles per hour, or sixty-four kilometres. During a work, they run at around thirty miles per hour. That's pretty fast when you're perched on a racehorse. If the horse ducks, dives, or stumbles, you're likely to fly off, risking serious injury.

We had eight horses in training. Sandy would tack a horse, then give me a leg up on it. While I was out galloping, he'd clean that horse's stall. One morning, after about forty days of conditioning, Sandy tossed me up on the first horse and then said, as he led the horse out of the barn, "Work him a half mile. These horses all need a work today."

Horses are like any athlete—you train them in increments, going longer and harder until they reach racing fitness. For a half-mile work, the horse would lope slowly for a mile, which was three laps of our little track, and then race fast around both turns, before loping slowly again for another lap of the track and then pulling up and walking home.

"Can't we take them in and work them at the racetrack?" I asked as I reached down to tighten my girth. "I'm not comfortable working them here."

"We don't have time to haul them all in. They need a work. So get to it."

My fear of getting dumped off overcame my reluctance to grovel. "I'm really not comfortable working them here. I seriously don't want to do it. Please, let's take them to the track?"

Sandy gave me the look. A look that was normally sufficient to shut me up and make me obey.

"I'm not doing it," I said, almost under my breath, testing the waters. I didn't want to argue loudly enough that the boys would hear me and be frightened by our conversation.

"What did you say?"

Bolder now, I spoke up. "This is stupid. It's asking for trouble. I'm not working them here!"

"The fuck you aren't!"

Sandy rushed toward me, and the gelding I was on skittered away from him. Gathering control of my horse, I shouted, "Fuck you! If you want them worked, you do it!" I turned my horse around and headed back into the barn and into its stall, where I jumped down and started to pull my saddle off.

Bam. Sandy's hand slammed into my back as he grabbed me from behind. My helmet flew off. The horse bolted past me out the door. Sandy dragged me by the scruff of the neck into the centre area of the barn. By this time, I was crying and screaming. "I'm scared to work them! I'm scared!" My head rattled as he shook me. "I won't do it."

We always hung water pails outside the horses' stalls, so they could reach out for a drink. Sandy dragged me over to a full water pail and shoved my head into it. Pulling my head out again, he snarled, "Are you going to work them?"

"No," I screamed as I gasped for breath, "I'm not!"

I clawed and fought as he shoved my head back under the water.

Out again. I sputtered, "I'm not doing it!"

Back underwater, Sandy shaking me. "Did you hear me! Answer me! Holly! You will work these horses! There's one boss here, and it's not you!"

Terrified, I realized I had blacked out under the water.

When Sandy released me, I slumped onto a hay bale, crying. He walked out the barn door, coming back moments later with the horse in tow. "Get on," he ordered.

I worked the horses that day. I worked them hard. I pushed on past the mares in the field, almost wanting one to charge me. I wasn't afraid anymore. I just didn't care.

Sandy was jovial and friendly afterwards. "Great job working the horses today," he said.

I loathed him. And I felt ashamed of myself when I went to let the boys out of their box stall. I knew they must have heard the fighting. I hadn't checked in on them once during the time it took to work all the horses. I'd been so caught up in my own emotions, I had left them all alone, and probably afraid. I gave them each a hug. "Hey, you guys. How are you doing in here? What do you say we go for a wiener roast?" My cure for everything was a wiener roast with the boys while Sandy stayed in the house watching TV.

❧

After the water bucket incident I lost my fear of climbing on a horse's back. I no longer worried about getting hurt. Maybe I was defying the odds. Riding fast horses became my escape from the reality of marriage to Sandy. It became my drug of choice.

Sandy and I both worked hard, and our horse-racing business flourished. Sandy had a great eye for horses. He made most of the decisions about which horses to buy, where to race them, and what their training protocol should be. He was one of the best farriers I'd ever seen, too. He had a natural feel for the way a shoe should fit on a horse's foot. That's crucial with racehorses. If they aren't shod correctly, they'll get sore or injured when they train and race. Shoeing can make or break a horse.

Sandy was very intelligent in all the business aspects of his life. There was nothing he couldn't figure out on the farm, whether it was equipment or livestock. His motivation to continually improve things was all-consuming. He carried us along with him. He and I worked well together, each with our own particular talents, and despite the fact I'd come to fear and mistrust him, part of me still loved him for his good qualities. When he turned on the charm, I couldn't help but be attracted to him. His techniques of punishment and reward worked well in his training of me. I struggled mightily for those small crumbs of positive reinforcement.

Sandy made friends easily. There was always a honeymoon phase, during which he was smitten by everything about his new acquaintance. As time progressed, he decided he either loved that person or hated them; there was no in-between. I was relieved that he had a lot of friends. They made him feel good about himself, which made him less frantic and explosive at home.

I was the primary target for Sandy's rage, but Jason and Mat were next in line. It was second nature for me to make myself visible when he started in on one of the boys. I was like a killdeer pretending to have a broken wing, fluttering and floundering to lure predators away from its chicks. Sometimes my trick worked, but other times Sandy was determined to vent his spleen on whichever boy was his target. The three of us were always on red alert to his moods, hoping to anticipate his tantrums and dampen them before they got too violent.

On one trip to Grande Prairie, I bought a book about personality disorders and domestic violence in the bookstore at the mall. I avoided eye contact at the checkout, ashamed to have anyone think I was being mistreated. I hid the book from Sandy when I got home, knowing he would react badly if he saw it.

I'd started to keep a secret journal, which I consulted whenever I questioned my sanity. Had Sandy really been as off the wall as I thought? Was I overreacting? The litany of incidents I documented grew and grew. I also decided I would buy a voice-activated tape recorder to see if I could catch some audio evidence of Sandy's abuses. I had no objective other than to keep myself from slipping down the rabbit hole. It's very hard to keep a grip on normal when you're spinning in the vortex an illogical, unstable person can create. As disturbing as my recordings of his tantrums were, they were also comforting. They reminded me that I wasn't imagining Sandy's behaviour. That allowed me to distance myself from it.

I didn't ride as a jockey for a number of years after my boys were born. When it came time for one of our horses to race, Sandy and I would hire a jockey to ride it. But in July 1989, when Matthew was six years old and Jason was nearly eight, I went back to race riding.

I'd been a full-time jockey in 1979 and 1980, and when I started race riding again, I discovered it was like riding a bicycle: once you learn how, you never forget. I was among the top riders everywhere I raced. In Grande Prairie the following July, I managed twenty-three wins in a sixteen-day period, including five wins in one day. Sandy was in Edmonton with our main stable at that time. The boys and I were racing our B string in Grande Prairie. I'd phone and tell Sandy how they ran, but we never spoke of my riding, although I'm sure he heard about it from others. There had been some gender-based discrimination when I first started race riding, but by 1989 I was on an equal basis with the men in pretty much every way. Most trainers at the racetrack had evolved to judge riders strictly on ability. If you could do the job you were respected and in demand.

To make riding weight for a jockey, around 117 pounds with saddle, many riders have to shake twenty or more pounds. Their lives are a constant merry-go-round of dieting. I never had to diet to maintain a body weight of a hundred and five pounds, and I often carried lead weights in my saddle pad to make up the difference. I didn't ride all season like most riders do either. Since I spent much of the year on the farm breaking horses, I could enjoy myself without the stress of burnout. I was lucky and I loved my job. When I was up on a horse's back, I was free. I didn't have to think about anything else.

By excelling once more as a jockey, I got a lot of my self-esteem back. I still had to watch myself, though, and be cautious I didn't ever cross the elusive line in the sand Sandy had drawn for me. He bombarded me constantly with degrading, belittling words and actions. His foul behaviour was designed to force me to fight back or break down, but I chose not to react unless it was impossible to avoid it. Often, if Sandy couldn't get a reaction from me, he would attack Jason or Matthew and draw me into his game when I defended them.

I had talked to my boys about Sandy's anger from the time they were toddlers, explaining that I couldn't change or control their father's conduct. His behaviour was not normal or acceptable, I made clear, "But we just have to deal with it. There are no other options." I was certain Sandy would find a way to make me pay if I took the boys and left. They were my most vulnerable point, and I protected them the best I knew how.

There were so many great facets to our life on the farm, that I often managed to blank out the bad things. Jason and Mat played on organized sports teams, went skiing, had snowmobiles and quads, and owned racehorses—opportunities a lot of kids would never have. Our family had no money worries, and we were all in good health.

But, as well, I recognized the madness of our lives with Sandy. We had to analyze our actions from every angle, always wondering if something we were planning would set him off. One thing guaranteed to soothe him was positive input from people outside the family. I became adept at deflecting any praise that came my way, or my sons' way, and directing it toward Sandy instead. I tried to make him feel that we were grateful to him for enabling us to live so well and that he was responsible for any success we had.

It usually wasn't hard to feel rich in what I had. I didn't realize until much later that I was glossing over the abuse my sons were subjected to. I had been raised by parents who adored and supported me, but Jason and Matthew's filters were entirely different. They could not expect to be treated fairly or decently by their father. Although I worked to fill that gap, there was no way I could. I knew if I split up with Sandy we would have to move far away. Otherwise, without question, he would do the boys and me harm. And I knew I'd be walking away with nothing; he would never accept me taking anything more than the petty cash I had. The choice was to disappear, giving up our community and our lifestyle, or to stay, keep my blinkers on, and accept the dark side.

CHAPTER 7

IN THE FALL of 1994, Sandy and I gave up racing horses as a full-time business and started cattle ranching. I continued to break horses for other people, but the only horse racing we planned to do was a six-week stretch in the summer, when I would race horses in Grande Prairie. The fact that I rode well was a big boost to our income, so even though Sandy didn't like the attention I got as a jockey, he did like my paycheques.

As Jason and Matthew became distinct individuals, developing their own personalities, Sandy's desperate need to control us intensified. Luckily he was busy with our new cattle-ranching venture, so it was possible to steer clear of him much of the time. Our policy was to keep him happy doing his own thing so we could do ours.

In 1995, I was leading jockey for the Grande Prairie race meet. I was also responsible for a stable of horses, which we won a lot of races with that summer. Jason and Matthew, along with their teenage cousin Eldon, served as my grooms and barn crew.

As the summer of 1996 rolled around, my barn crew and I were excited about the upcoming race season. We had a great stable of horses lined up and we anticipated doing some serious winning again. However, we couldn't talk about racing with Sandy around. He was extremely sour about not being involved. Anytime anything to do with racing came up, he threw a tantrum of some sort. I tried to downplay things, but Jason, Matthew, and I were involved with the racing association, planning dances, pancake breakfasts, and other social activities that would occur during the race meet. There were phone calls and meetings that couldn't be kept on the QT.

The pressure was building, and I felt like something was about to give. Sandy was becoming more erratic and irrational.

I knew it would be useless to ask him to go for counselling. I remembered all too well how he reacted in the early years of our marriage when I tried that approach. But Sandy liked the man who had been our family doctor since before Jason was born, so I decided to ask him if he would meet with the two of us. Maybe Sandy wouldn't feel threatened if a suggestion came from our family doctor.

I called to set up an appointment. I didn't give our doctor a full account of Sandy's unpredictable and violent behaviour. I gave him just enough information that he could understand a bit of our dynamics. I had stayed silent for far too long to easily reveal the shameful situation at home. I felt massive, often overwhelming, shame. I didn't want anyone to know that my husband, who should be loving and protecting me, was hitting me, choking me, and spitting on me instead. Despite my reputation for being fearless in horse-racing circles, I felt weak and cowardly for tolerating Sandy's treatment of me.

During the meeting, our doctor told Sandy that his behaviour was not normal. He tried to subtly get Sandy to understand how negatively his violence was affecting our family. But when we left the doctor's office, Sandy was jubilant. For some reason, he felt that the doctor had been impressed with him. He stuck his tongue out at me, did a joyous little skip, then twirled down the sidewalk as we walked toward our truck, giggling and taunting me with, "*Nah nah, nah nah nah.*"

Once we got in the truck, his silly mood evaporated, and I knew I was in trouble. Sandy's face reddened, and his tongue curled out between his teeth. Suddenly, his hand shot out, and he grabbed my ear. Twisting it, he pulled me toward him until I was inches away, then he spat in my face. My body clenched as he snarled, "Even the doc thinks your problems are all in your head. You better quit being so selfish and start thinking of me for a change!"

My head bounced off the passenger side window when he flung me away from him. My ear was burning, my head throbbing, my stomach churning. I slumped against the door, leaning as far away from him as I could. He slammed the truck in gear and pulled away from the curb. I found a tissue in my pocket and used it to mop the slime from my face.

I knew I had to do something. I just wasn't sure what. I had a stable full of horses and two young sons I was responsible for. I couldn't just pack my bags and leave.

A week later I went down in a spill on a racehorse called Gypsy Dancer, and my life changed forever.

PIONEERING JOCKEY SERIOUSLY INJURED

John Short, *Edmonton Journal*, July 10

Holly Crichton fell from horse-back or was thrown many times in a career that made her one of the best female riders in Canadian racing history. It happened again in a weekend event at Grande Prairie.

This tumble was shockingly, distressingly different.

The 38-year-old jockey didn't get up after her horse, Gypsy Dancer, clipped the heels of another horse at the first turn, causing a chain reaction pileup.

The sixth and seventh vertebrae of Crichton's spine were smashed.

Surgery was completed Monday at Edmonton's University Hospital.

"Holly has no feeling or movement from about the middle of her chest all the way to her feet," husband Sandy Crichton, a veteran thoroughbred trainer, said in a telephone conversation after the operation, "but she came out of the operation OK… She can't move from the chest down, but there is some movement in her hands and arms and shoulders."

As for a long-term prognosis, "They [the doctors] aren't telling us anything right now."

Later, a hospital official said the injured athlete is in stable condition.

Sandy was among approximately 500 spectators to witness the accident. "The track was muddy," he said. "But the mud didn't have anything to do with it."

"Her horse just bolted, that's all. He wasn't going to go around the turn. He was on the inside and when he tried to get out, he clipped the heels of another horse that was running outside of him."

Watching the incident unfold, Crichton recalled, "Before it actually happened, you could see something was going on."

"It looked like she was clear, that they were going to make it out of there. But at the last moment, they clipped and went down." The other horse was Rikollo, ridden by Carl Hebert, who escaped serious injury.

Gypsy Dancer broke a leg and was humanely destroyed.

"I thought Holly would bounce right back up," her husband said. "The way she always did."

Instead medical personnel moved toward her. She was taken to hospital near the track, then was transferred to the University Hospital's trauma unit.

The Crichtons have two sons, 13 and 15. Both are in Edmonton with their parents.

"Accidents happen," Sandy said carefully. "They're part of racing. Holly knew about the risks—she's been around the sport a long time—but she loved racing so much she just wanted to keep riding."

Holly's pro career started in 1979. Many women now riding on Canadian tracks owe something to such pioneers of the sport. Since 1994, she has been riding exclusively at Grande Prairie during the brief annual summer meet. For a few years previously, she made a habit of competing at Calgary and Edmonton late in the summer.

For the bulk of her career, Crichton was effective on Alberta's 'B' circuit, starting in spring and working through to fall, racing in the afternoon and riding numerous horses every morning. She also had some success in other western provinces. At one time or another she rode for many of the province's leading trainers.

Sandy and Holly met about 18 years ago, Sandy recalled, which means they were a team at Calgary's Stampede Park a few years ago when Holly won five races on a single thoroughbred card—a one-day performance matched in Canada by few, if any, female riders.

I felt very calm as I lay on my stomach on the racetrack, my mouth full of dirt. I could hear Riley Rycroft yelling, "Don't move her!" and Jackie Smith saying, "Check her mouth. She always chews gum." "Settle down, you guys," I wanted to say. "Just give me a minute here, and I'll bounce back up." Then blackness.

I moved in and out of consciousness as they loaded me into an ambulance. My mind was still calm, almost serene. *I'm going to die*, I thought, a bit surprised. *I'm so sorry, my boys. I'm so sorry…*

Then: *No, I will not die. I can't leave you alone.* Then blackness again.

I came to in ICU in the hospital in Edmonton, where I'd been flown by medevac. My parents, the doctors, and Sandy were all peering down at me. Suddenly, I had the weird sensation I was peering down at them. *I've caused everyone so much trouble*, I thought. *You'll be okay without me.* Then *no… I can't… I can't leave my boys.*

A neurosurgeon explained to me that my spinal cord was crushed and had a number of bone splinters in it. They'd have to operate and put rods along my spine to stabilize it. I gave my consent without fully grasping what he said. I could tell that Sandy was loving the attention he got from being my spokesman, talking to the press and fielding phone calls. I thought even then that it was ironic the world would see him as my champion.

About ten days after my wreck, when I finally came out of shock and didn't need as much morphine, I realized I'd been smashed like a bug on a sidewalk during my accident. Up until then, I'd been telling myself that I had to hurry up and get out of the hospital so I didn't lose too much condition. I thought that I might be able to ride the last part of the Grande Prairie race meet in August. At first, I couldn't comprehend that I was paralyzed.

But even with seven shattered ribs, two shattered vertebrae, a broken collarbone and two punctured lungs, my greatest worry was what I was going to do about Sandy. I could barely survive living with him as an able-bodied person. I didn't think I could make it as a paraplegic.

Sandy told me the nurses had asked him to keep people out of my room. Some of them ignored him and came in anyway, but I could hear him turning away many of my friends. Thoroughbred horse racing was still a thriving industry in those days, and lots of people I knew were at the races at Northlands Park in Edmonton for the summer meet. My sister and my parents refused to be pushed away, however, and one or the other of them was constantly at my side. Karen Boyce, an exercise rider I'd been friends with for years, and who had sustained a brain injury in a spill two years before, came to help me at the hospital nearly every day. She got me clothes to wear, did my laundry, and brought me healthy food for the whole time I was hospitalized.

After some time, I was moved to the Glenrose Rehabilitation Hospital in Edmonton. A number of therapists worked with me there, including a psychologist whose job it was to help me adjust to my new reality. I admitted to her that my main concern was life with Sandy: I didn't think I could survive it. I told my parents and a few close friends the same thing. The only person who'd known about my home life up until then was my friend Ruth Finch. She had worked in social services, and a few years earlier I'd gone to her looking for advice.

After I got hurt, Sandy went in occasionally to help Mat and Eldon look after our stable at the racetrack, and he did the haying at home by himself. Jason hadn't wanted to come to the racetrack with us, so he'd begun working on a farm a few miles from ours. On one of his visits to the Glenrose, I told him I couldn't go back to the farm, and he said he understood. Some women friends from Grande Prairie, along with members of the Grovedale women's hockey team I played with, offered me help with finding a place to live, and they started planning a fundraiser for me.

When I phoned Sandy to say I was leaving him, he got nasty and told me I could forget about seeing the boys ever again. But soon he changed tactics, begging me to come home. I hadn't seen Mat since just after my accident, and Sandy agreed to bring him for a visit. As they were leaving, I told Mat I couldn't go back to the farm. He started to cry, and Sandy ordered him out of my hospital room, cursing me over his shoulder.

A month after my accident, the horse-racing community in Edmonton hosted a fundraising dinner and dance for me at

Northlands Park. Sandy phoned me to ask what he should wear. He laughed when I told him he wasn't welcome to come.

But as time went on, I realized what a terrible predicament I was in. What would I do to earn a living? And what would happen to my children? The only job I'd ever had, other than weekends and after school when I'd worked as the cook's flunky at the Douglas Lake cookhouse, was riding horses. I had no skills that would allow me to earn enough as a paraplegic to support myself and the boys. I felt overwhelming guilt about getting hurt and complicating life so much more than it already had been.

Jason, Mat, and I could move to my parents' place at Valemount, where my father had already set to work making one of the cabins wheelchair accessible for me. But I knew Sandy would go out of his way to sabotage me and make things as tough as possible. In the end, I chose to go back to the farm, thinking that staying there would be the best choice for my boys. They wouldn't have to give up their quality of life, and my amazing group of friends in the Grande Prairie area had offered to be my support team as I made the transition to life in a wheelchair.

Sandy was great for a while after I returned home, but soon the veneer wore off his nice-guy act, and we were back to the bizarre ups and downs of daily life. Only now, I was more trapped than ever before. You learn as a rider that the way to deal with a runaway horse is to ride it out, not bail off. The odds of making it through the situation unscathed, without causing a wreck all around you, are a lot higher if you don't panic; you just keep steering around the obstacles until your horse tires out. The same seemed true of my life with Sandy. I convinced myself that bailing off would be a lot more dangerous than riding it out. *Keep your friends close and your enemies closer,* I thought.

As time went on, I watched helpless as Mat would come in crying after Sandy hit him with a pitchfork, or threw him down in the snow. Jason never cried or said a word when Sandy hit him, he just did his best to do chores without Sandy around so he didn't have to work with him. The boys were both playing hockey that winter, and Sandy rode them hard, yelling commands constantly while they were on the ice, and berating them in the van on the way to and from the arena. I wasn't able to drive yet, so I sat on my wheelchair in the back of the van while Sandy drove.

The staff at the Glenrose had told me that my therapy once I got home would be looking after myself; that would take all my energy, they said. I was frustrated at how utterly useless I was, but thankfully a never-ending stream of friends and neighbours stepped up constantly to help me with everything from stretching my legs to grocery shopping and cleaning house. My hockey team even tried putting me in goal in my wheelchair, though we soon learned that that wouldn't work well. I felt the worst about not being able to defend my sons, however, and I wondered if they'd be better off without me. We seemed to have lost our connection, and they felt distant from me. When Sandy ordered them to do things for me, I knew they resented it. But before long the dark curtain that had held us apart evaporated. I realized my boys needed me to be their mom even if I couldn't physically do anything for them.

❦

I rode thoroughbred racehorses every night in my dreams. In the dreams I sat in a special saddle that held me in a bunched-up position, perched like a butterfly on a horse's back. I was powerful. Graceful. Weightless. Every morning when I woke, I thought if I could just get up onto a horse's back I'd be me again, not this terrible leaden body that felt like it was encased in concrete.

That summer I got a special western-style saddle made, with a high back and Velcro straps to tie me onto it. I also met a cowboy named Ray Strom, who said, "I have the perfect horse for you to ride." He gave me a great old ranch horse named Junior.

The first time I got up on Junior, just over a year after I'd gone down in the spill that broke my back, my disappointment was profound. I was still a block of unfeeling concrete, only now I was perched high off the ground, feeling dizzy and afraid.

All the people who'd helped me get up on that horse had gathered for the occasion. They were standing around with big grins on their faces, excited and happy for me. There was no way I could let them all down. I had to suck it up and ride.

Junior truly was a fabulous horse. Only moments before, he had been doing sliding stops and rollbacks with Ray on his back. Now, as I asked him to go by jiggling the reins and clucking at him, he walked gingerly around the barnyard bearing me.

After a few weeks, my friends Donna and Sherry asked if I'd teach their kids to ride. They each had a son born in 1983, the same age as Matthew, and the kids were in the same class at our local country school. Donna and Sherry each had a younger daughter as well, so once Matthew joined us, along with our neighbours Frank and Lorna Gould's daughter, I had a group of six riders.

In return for the lessons, Donna and Sherry did various maintenance jobs around our house and yard. We spent most of the summer working together. Their presence, and my welcome new role as a teacher, made me forget about my limitations.

CHAPTER 8

SHORTLY AFTER I got home from the Glenrose, Sandy and I had bought a used wheelchair-accessible van. A year later, the Workers' Compensation Board acknowledged that since I had been paying for personal coverage under horseracing, they were obligated to insure me. They paid for a brand-new, wheelchair-equipped van and began to supply any other medical aids and accessories I needed. They completely remodelled our house to make it accessible and began paying me a monthly pension. Now I could at least pay my own way again.

When my horse, Junior, died of unknown causes, I bought a three-year-old filly to replace him. She was too rough for me, though, so I sold her and bought a young gelding. He turned out to be too green. After a few scary rides on him, I decided to sell him too, which meant I no longer had a saddle horse.

Soon I had a new direction to explore, however: painting with watercolours. My friend Joyce Balisky brought artist Jim Adrian out to teach me how to paint, and I was hooked as I watched him perform magic with his paints. He started coming to the farm every Tuesday, leaving me lesson instructions and bits of scrap watercolour paper to practise on. Then he would critique my work the following week. Sadly, one morning I got a call that Jim had suffered a massive heart attack and died. Only when I went to his funeral did I realize what a popular and respected artist he was. I kept practising on my own. I won a few local competitions, and for a number of years afterwards I participated in art shows throughout Alberta. The physical toll of travel became too much for me, so I eventually quit showing, though I continued to paint.

Jason graduated from high school in 1999 and moved into an apartment in Grande Prairie with two roommates. He took computer systems training at the college there, and worked part-time, coming out to the farm to help whenever we needed a hand. In 2001 he moved to Edmonton to work in a lumberyard and take classes at the Northern Alberta Institute of Technology. Mat graduated from high school the same year and started training horses in Grande Prairie.

One morning as Sandy and I were having breakfast, he banged his cup on the table, signalling me that he wanted a refill. He hadn't done that for a long time, and I could see that he was looking for a fight. When I ignored him, he banged his cup harder and harder, finally flinging it at me as he unleashed his usual curses and accusations.

As his cup bounced off my shoulder, I thought, *That's it. Matti and Jason are on their own now. I'm leaving.* Sandy could have the farm. It wasn't worth the price I had to pay for putting up with him.

I knew that a week later, when the Grande Prairie races were over, Sandy would be helping Mat move his horses to Edmonton. He would be gone overnight, so I made plans to leave while he was away. Two friends came out and spent the afternoon loading my little bumper-pull trailer with all my paraphernalia: wheelchairs, shower chair, commode chair, medical supplies, art supplies, farm books, dog food, blankets, and clothing. Early the next morning, I loaded my two dogs, Lady and Gyp, into my van and hit the road. I was terrified as I drove away from home. I knew Sandy would be furious with me for leaving. He wasn't expected home until that evening; what if something happened and he caught me? I could easily see him running my van off the road with his truck.

I headed to my parents' place at Valemount. They weren't surprised to hear that Sandy hadn't changed, and they were prepared to do anything they could to help me out. I was planning to go and live with my cousin Jaydah in southern BC. Sandy would never think to look for me there, but all of us were nervous he might show up at Mom and Dad's during the night. I phoned Jason to tell him I was going into hiding and asked him to let Mat know. I had an uneasy sleep in my van, and first thing in the morning I hit the road again.

That fall, I ended up going from Jaydah's place in Grand Forks to Sherwood Park, near Edmonton, where I moved in with my racetrack friends Lyle Peterson and Wendy Kadar. Over time, Sandy and I agreed on a settlement; my lawyer told me I was a fool to settle for so little, but I just wanted to be free of Sandy. He'd promised he would keep the farm intact for the boys. I continued to do the farm's books, because I always had, and I didn't want to cause any more disruption. The following spring, as the time we'd agreed upon to sign separation papers grew nearer, Sandy began phoning more often, begging me to come home. I kept refusing, and finally he said, "If you don't come back, I'll have another cook in here so fast your head will spin. You guys will be out for good. If you think I'm holding onto this place for those boys, you can think again. You get home, or the boys get nothing."

That was a moment of enlightenment for me. I realized Sandy couldn't care less if I lived in a cardboard box under a bridge, or whether the boys had a farm to come home to, as long as he got what he wanted. It was as if my vision cleared, and I saw that it wasn't about me at all. I was just a tool in Sandy's toolbox, and the farm was a lever he used to control the boys and me. I felt the hurt lift off my shoulders. This was simply business.

Mat had gone off to farrier school in Oklahoma, and when he got back to Grande Prairie, where he was staying with friends, he called me one evening. "Mom, I really miss the farm and I don't want to lose it. Is there any way we can go back there?"

Mat and Jay could have gone out to the farm anytime, but they didn't want to be there alone with Sandy. After Mat's call, I made the choice once again to return to the farm.

With Jason in Edmonton, and Mat busy following the racing circuit during the summer, Sandy and I fell back into the old routine of working together for the good of the farm. Sandy was proud of Mat because of Mat's good reputation at the racetrack and on the chuckwagon racing circuit, and he welcomed him home for the winter, in between race seasons.

On January 29, 2004, a dreaded phone call came at a time of night when phones shouldn't ring.

The phone was on the kitchen wall, so Sandy answered it. From his voice, I knew something was bad. He hung up and told me.

"That was Nicholas Hansen. Matti and Derek Lofstrom had a car wreck."

"Oh, fuck. Oh, fuck. Oh, fuck." I tried to scramble up but went into a spasm. Sandy chastised me for swearing.

When we finally got to my van, my wheelchair rims were full of snow and my pants were soaked. Sandy drove while I sat on my chair in the back. I wasn't thinking about anything. My mind had gone blank.

We saw flashing lights far ahead in the black, black night. Our van was still freezing. The heater hadn't even warmed it up yet, and it was thirty below outside. I couldn't stop shivering.

Then, the shattered car appeared in our headlights. I saw our neighbour JoAnne Bremner sitting in a pile of mangled metal. She was cradling Matthew's head. He was pinned.

Matthew was flown by air ambulance from the Grande Prairie hospital to the University of Alberta's brain trauma unit in Edmonton. Sandy phoned Jason, who went to the hospital to await Mat's arrival. Sandy, Brian Lofstrom, and Derek's sister Amber stayed to feed the cows in the morning. Sherry Lofstrom, Derek, and I headed out in my van in a blizzard at four in the morning, with five hundred kilometres of road ahead of us. My bladder was chilled and it released. I changed my clothes in the back of the van while Sherry drove. Wearing clean, dry, yoga pants and an adult diaper, I took a turn driving. We saw semis in the ditch as we passed. We crawled by them, hoping we were still on the highway. Derek slept in the back of the van, but he woke up on the outskirts of Edmonton and took over driving from there.

The previous evening, Derek, Matthew's best friend since childhood, had been driving home from a movie in his mother's car with Matthew in the passenger seat. Matthew's side of the car was struck head-on by an oilfield truck that had lost control on glare ice. Derek, an athletic twenty-year-old who played organized hockey and baseball and wrestled at the university level, wasn't injured, and he'd managed to escape from the car while Matthew lay trapped and unconscious. The Grovedale Volunteer Fire Department had arrived within minutes, followed shortly by Grande Prairie Emergency Services.

In the days that followed, we learned that Mat had a crushed right femur, a broken right ankle, and a shattered right wrist.

His jaw was broken in two places. He also had an "Extremely Severe Traumatic Brain Injury," scoring a 3 on what's known as the Glasgow Coma Scale: as low as you could go and not be brain dead, the doctors told us.

I grieved for Mat as if he had died, because that's how it felt to me, as if the Matthew I knew would no longer be inside his body if and when he woke up. As I sat with him in ICU over the next few weeks, I read books from the university library about injuries like his. I learned the odds of him coming through with his old personality were very low. I experienced the same surreal sense of confusion as when I was injured myself. The world went on as normal, while my reality was completely shattered. Everyone was concerned, and involved, and helpful, but they continued with their everyday lives, while first me, and now Matthew, would never experience normal again.

On January 31, forty-eight hours after Mat's accident, Dr. Pugh, the neurosurgeon, showed us some CAT scans. If Mat's brain continued to swell, Dr. Pugh explained, he would be considered brain dead. He asked if Matthew had signed an organ donor card. I told him I didn't think so, but assured him we would make the decision for Mat to donate, if it came to that.

When I'd been in the ICU after my accident, I'd drawn strength from people touching me. I often didn't know who was there, but I could feel the energy coming through their hands, and it helped me immensely. I vowed to provide Matthew with as much positive energy as he could get, from me and from anyone else who was there to give it to him.

While Mat was in the hospital, I was allowed to stay in one of the rooms normally reserved for transplant patients. I had a never-ending stream of roommates in my drafty little room. My sister Bobbi was there with me, just as she'd been when I got hurt. She spent hours at Mat's bedside. Sandy came down regularly, but we had a herd of cows to look after at home.

The next few weeks were filled with giddy highs and crushing lows. On many occasions Mat teetered on the edge of death, then fought back and surged upward again. The surgeons had not dealt with the other injuries to Mat's body at first, since his brain couldn't cope with more stress. The delay caused more complications as bone marrow seeped into his blood stream from his shattered femur and worked its way, along with blood clots, to his lungs. If he survived, the doctors told us, there was an overwhelming likelihood that he would be profoundly disabled. I realized he might not even get well enough to return to the farm he loved so much.

On February 22, Sherry and Derek Lofstrom and I were sitting with Matthew in his hospital room when we saw the first spark that he was comprehending what anyone said. We had been teasing him about his long toes as he lay unconscious, and all of a sudden he grinned. Next, Derek said that he was going out with the university wrestling team that night, and would have a shot of tequila for Matthew. Mat grinned more widely. His eyes were still closed, but he was connecting with us after three weeks of nothing.

Throughout the gruelling process of Matthew's long hospitalization and rehabilitation, Derek was there to support him. A better friend could not be imagined. Derek's father, Brian Lofstrom, had known Sandy his entire life. His father had often shared equipment or labour with Sandy, and so did Brian once he started farming on his own. Sandy was a mentor and a friend to him. Brian was around five foot nine, with a thick shock of salt-and-pepper hair and a rangy, fat-free frame. Always on the go, he was a natural athlete who excelled at everything he did, from trapping and hunting to playing ball or hockey to taking a crop of grain off the field.

Sherry and I had been friends since our children were babies. We'd played hockey together on the Hockey Bags team, and we spent countless hours socializing as we took kids to practices, games, on school field trips, and to fundraising events. After my accident, I'd become as close to Sherry as I was to my own sister. She helped me learn to cope with my paralysis. Matti's accident with her son Derek would bring us even closer. Sherry was petite and elegant, a warm, beautiful person inside and out. She was equally comfortable in dress clothes at an art show, in her volunteer fire fighter's uniform on an emergency call, and in her coveralls helping to calve a cow in distress. She was a true pillar of the community.

After a month in the university hospital, Mat was sent to the Grande Prairie hospital for another month, while awaiting a bed at the Glenrose Rehab Centre. He slowly started to improve, but still functioned at a very low level.

Sandy didn't want Mat to go to the Glenrose. He kept insisting that Mat was fine and should be sent directly home. I was terrified that Mat's doctor would concede to Sandy's pressure, and simply release him. When I explained my fears, our family doctor immediately became proactive in finding Mat a bed at the Glenrose. He was sent there by medevac, and the staff began intensive physical and mental therapy with him.

I hadn't realized Mat's vision was impaired until the intake doctor pointed it out to me. She explained it was common for people suffering from brain injuries to have severe vision damage as well. A motel near the hospital gave me a cut-rate room, and I stayed in Edmonton to help with Mat's rehab. Jason came to the Glenrose regularly, and he sometimes took Mat and me for meals at the downtown apartment where he lived.

A long, hard grind lay ahead for Matthew, but he never felt sorry for himself, and he never quit trying. Our local community and friends and family near and far were there for him. That support played a major role in the remarkable recovery he made.

During Mat's hospitalization and rehab, Sandy looked after the farm by himself, feeding and calving the cows, then seeding a crop in the spring. Immediately after Mat's accident, we had sold a hundred first-calf heifers at a great loss. The dreaded BSE disease had hit the fall before and cattle were nearly worthless, but Sandy couldn't look after calving two hundred head by himself.

Sandy was very supportive of Mat in the early days after his accident, when Mat was as helpless as a newborn baby. Then, just as he had done when Jason and Mat began as young children to have minds of their own, as Mat began to recover Sandy got agitated. Rather than support Mat in becoming independent, he insisted on treating him like an invalid. He fought me at every turn when I pushed Mat to do things for himself, mocking sarcastically, "Oh, you think you're the expert now? Should I call you Doctor Holl*eeee*? You know how to do *evereee*ything!"

A couple of months after Mat's injury, while he was awaiting admittance to the Glenrose brain rehab unit, Sandy and I reached a point where we could no longer be in Matti's hospital room at the same time without me burning with fury. Mat was beginning to feed himself at that point. The nurses set his tray in front of him, propped him up and gave him a spoon. Only about half the food made it to his mouth, but he was doing it on his own. I arrived at his room one lunchtime to find Sandy spoon-feeding him. The look in Mat's eyes almost broke my heart; he looked like a trapped animal, unable to speak or to stand up for himself. I knew he took great pride in the steps he was making toward recovery, and having his father insist on spoon-feeding him was a blow to that sense of accomplishment.

"He can do that by himself, you know?" I said to Sandy cautiously. "It's really important that Mat learn to be as independent as possible. That's why the nurses set his tray up the way they do."

He glared at me as he continued to spoon the pureed food into Mat, making little pucker faces like people do when they feed babies. "Well, I like feeding him," he said belligerently.

On May 1, our friends and neighbours organized a benefit fundraiser for Mat in Grande Prairie. As the local paper, the *Daily Herald Tribune*, reported:

> For those who know him, Mat Crichton was always the guy everyone could depend on to help out… Whether it was casinos, or fundraisers, or getting ready for the races, Mat loved to lend a hand. Last year, he even went to Oklahoma to take training in horseshoeing so that he could do that for the park.
>
> A good deed done deserves a good deed in turn. Now it's the community's turn to help Mat… At the end of this month, the people he always helped will give back with a benefit in his honour, with a garage sale from April 29 to May 1 and a dinner and silent/live auction on May 1…
>
> Mat has now taken more steps than anyone had ever thought. As of last week he was finally able to get on to crutches. But it's the neurological injuries which are affecting him most. Just as if he had had a stroke, his right side isn't working properly. Mat has to learn to read and write again, and his vision has been affected. Even his speech isn't quite right. He gets his words

mixed up, such as he might want a toothbrush but will ask for a mirror…

Mat is now at the Glenrose trying to recover. Him being there gives his mother Holly confidence. She knows they're among the best at what they do because she's been there before.

In July 1996, Holly took a spill while riding and was left paralyzed from the chest down. She spent three months at the Glenrose and she has never forgotten how the people there helped her.

"Everybody there has either a brain or spinal cord injury and they show you that you just have to go on with your life and they teach you how to deal with it."

The event raised a whopping $62,000 toward Mat's rehab costs. He was deeply touched by the outpouring of support, and so was I. "Pretty good sign how much everyone loves you Mat," wrote our friend Ruth Finch in an e-mail. I opened an account for Matthew and put the money in it.

The Glenrose therapists had wanted Mat to be transferred to the Ponoka Institution for more therapy at the end of April, but I felt he would progress better at home with the support of his friends and community. And Mat was desperate to get home to the farm.

When he was discharged, I was given a list of tasks to continue with him. Before his accident, Mat had been an avid reader; now he had to learn to read again, and that was complicated by his vision problems. He also had to overcome neurological and physical damage in order to walk. Everyone in the community went out of their way to include him, and he slowly began to improve and connect with reality again.

Mat lived in the farmhouse with Sandy and me. The BSE cattle crisis had hit our bottom line hard, and Sandy wanted to use the money in Mat's account to invest in farm improvements. I felt it was crucial for Mat to have his own dwelling. I thought it would not be healthy for him to have to live with us forever, even if he might never be able to be completely on his own. So in the summer of 2005, at my insistence, we used Mat's money to buy a second-hand mobile home and have it set up close to our house.

We had an addition built on one side and a porch with a large deck on the other. The windows were upgraded, and then the entire dwelling was re-sided. The renos made it look like a cute little bungalow. To complete his yard, we set up a little chicken house with a dozen laying hens in it.

Once Matthew's residence was set up, we used the remaining money from the fundraiser to construct a shop for him, two hundred metres north of his house. An outdoor wood-burning furnace was installed in the yard, with underground water lines piped to the house and the shop for heat. At the southwest corner of his shop, Mat built a straw bale outhouse. Making it was a huge job for him. He still wasn't physically or mentally capable of much, and he struggled day after day to accomplish the job. Using tools, making plans, and completing the task of building the outhouse was wonderful rehab for him.

Matthew improved noticeably for about two years after his accident, then levelled off at a point where he still had disabilities but was able to function on his own and be productive. He was termed by medical professionals as a semi-dependent adult. Before his accident, Mat had made a name for himself as a farrier at the racetrack and on the chuckwagon racing circuit. Now he was grateful to be able to hit a nail accurately on one out of three tries, never mind hammering a shoe onto a fidgeting thoroughbred's foot. He contented himself with puttering about in his new shop, making small craft items for friends and for fundraisers.

CHAPTER 9

As he grew healthier, Mat resumed helping around the farm. For the first year, the most he could do was hold tools and open gates for Sandy. He was like a robot, following whatever orders his father gave him. He never tried to think for himself or offered an opinion, which suited Sandy. Although he slept in his new home, Mat was not capable of making his own meals, so he ate with us.

Sandy continued his abusive treatment of me and, to maintain my sanity, I recorded the worst incidents in my secret journal.

Journal entry: September 13, 2005, 3:31 a.m.

Sandy used to get teased at the track in Edmonton. It seemed that when the boys and I got to Edmonton every year after the Grande Prairie race meet was over, Sandy's horses would start winning races. People would be joking around, saying things like "Well, your horses should start running now, Holly's here!" It was just good-natured teasing, but they didn't realize how it ate at him. He took it as an insult.

I decided a few months ago to get a couple of older racehorses to take to the track next summer, partly because I think it'll be good for me to get involved again and partly because I think it'll be good for Mat. He's become a hermit since his accident. He can't seem to reconnect with life. I hope that since he was a racetracker all his life he'll fit back into the racetrack environment, and it'll help him connect the dots.

I didn't want to say anything about my plans to Sandy, but I pretty much had to. I knew that it would become a battle. The other morning it started to come out of him. He commented a few times in a derogatory way, "Oh! The big hot-shot horse trainers! Well, we'll see about that, we'll see." Then snickered to himself.

Another morning he popped out with the comment, "I'll have to take a few horses in to the track, and we'll see who the real trainer is." It's so disgusting. I can see him moving into the same shed row as us and taking all our stuff, even making us look after his horses. If they do well, it will be all about his training, and if not, it will be our fault. He doesn't get it that the main purpose is rehab for Matti, not so I can go back to the racetrack.

Journal entry: November 7, 2005, 8:31 p.m.

My mom fell out of bed and broke her neck. She's 85 years old and weighs about 90 lbs. Mat went to Peace River with me for an art show, and we stayed overnight there last night. I didn't have a phone with me, so I didn't know about Mom until I got home this morning. As soon as I heard, I began making arrangements to go to Kamloops, where Mom is. Dad is staying there at the hospital guest rooms. He said he'll get us a room, too, so we can be with him. He hurt his hip two weeks ago. He didn't tell me— my sister did, and she said he's really sore.

Mat, Sandy and I were having lunch today when I asked Mat if he was up for another road trip. Sandy immediately flipped out. He bellowed at me, "There's no way Mat can go. He has to help me hang gates and put equipment away!"

I know Mat has a lot he wants to do at home, so maybe I shouldn't ask him to come with me. I also know that Mat cares very much about his grandmother and would likely want to see her one last time. I really want someone with me, too. It's a concern for me driving through the mountains in winter. If I break down, my cellphone won't work through the pass. I'd be in a bad spot with my wheelchair, pretty hard to hitchhike. I've decided to leave it up to Mat.

Journal entry: November 8, 2005, 9:20 a.m.

This morning Mat came in and said he's decided to go with me. Sandy went goofy again, yelling about how Mat can't think for himself and I can't do anything for myself, yelling that nobody ever thinks about him. He said it's too bad Mom broke her neck but that people get what they deserve in this life. He said she's lived her life, and she's going to die anyway, so what difference will it make if we're there or not?

I couldn't believe he would say something like that. I said, "If you were lying there dying, wouldn't you want people who love you to be with you?"

That stumped him a bit, then he started whining, "Well, I'd like to go visiting too, but I have to stay home and do everything here. I always have to."

Mat said to him, "When I get back, you can go visiting."

Sandy pouted and stomped, shouting, "No! I want to go *right now!*"

He doesn't comprehend that going to sit with my dying mother and be there for my dad is not the same as going visiting. He then said to me, "You don't even know what real love is!"

I asked him, "What do you think 'real love' is?"

He said, "Not like the way you use the word to get what you want, or to get people to do things for you. Love should be something you show by the way you act."

JOURNAL ENTRY: NOVEMBER 8, 2005, 9:37 P.M.

By this afternoon Sandy was acting jolly and happy, trying to be friendly and cute one minute and the next second walking around muttering sarcastically to himself, "I don't know what's coming out of my mouth." (I'd said to him that he couldn't possibly know what he's saying, to say the things he does.)

Mat had an appointment to get his jaw clamps adjusted today, so we decided to go to his appointment and head for Kamloops first thing tomorrow morning.

I like to watch *Law and Order* while I do my hour of assisted walking exercise every night. Last night it was about this guy who murdered his son's hockey coach because the coach benched his kid. The defence lawyers tried to argue that it was "Sports Rage" and the man should be innocent of wrongdoing because of mental defect. They said he was so incensed by the coach that he had no idea what he was doing. The defence didn't work, and the guy got charged with murder.

When the show ended, Sandy started muttering. "Just like it's inexcusable to slam doors, *hee hee hee*. Some people think they can make excuses and get away with stuff." It makes the hair stand up on the back of my neck when he does that creepy little chuckle.

He was reminding me that he has a very long memory, going back to the early days of our marriage. I once slammed a door when we were having an argument. At the time, Sandy chased me and choked me down, screaming at me that I'd better not be slamming any doors in his house. He reminds me of it every once in a while, just to make sure I know he hasn't forgotten.

He turns it on and off like a light switch. He sees himself as the innocent victim of bad behaviour (usually mine). You could argue that he's insane, the way he bounces from euphoria to rage and back again, but he always assures me that he knows exactly what he's saying and doing. So, I would guess he's perfectly sane but gets some sort of enjoyment out of his bizarre, radical behaviour.

When I was first with Sandy, he would look in the mirror and say, "I'm such a good-looking guy." I used to think he was just being a smartass, but I eventually realized he was serious. He still does it. Last night his remark was, "I'm such a good-looking guy—if only I wasn't so fat." Normally he doesn't put in the part about being too fat, so it must be bothering him.

I read many abused-wife books in the early years, and one thing they said was that the abuser has very low self-esteem. Theoretically, if you could make them feel good about themselves, they'd lose the need to abuse others. I tried that, but the more I complimented Sandy the more arrogant and abusive he got. I think he believed he was doing me a huge favour by being with me, since I was a loser and he was so great. In fact, he's told me that on hundreds of occasions.

JOURNAL ENTRY: NOVEMBER 9, 2005, 8:35 A.M.

Mat and I are taking off this morning for Kamloops. Sandy's been all chummy for the most part, though every once in a while he goes off on me because I'm not playing his game. I'm supposed to play by the rules, which means he can go into his insane rages and do all his name-calling and threatening (he throws in any-thing he can think of, and he has a pretty nasty mind). Then, when he's got that out of his system for the moment, he feels happy and relieved and everyone else is supposed to respond to that. It leaves us all shaky and upset. I remember one of the boys telling me when he was very young: "Dad sucks all my energy."

I don't like myself much when I'm being a bitch. I pretty much ignore him, other than to answer his direct questions, but my habit has always been to be angry for a while and then let it go. That plays right into his game, and he's never held respon-sible. In fact, he turns it around so in his mind it was *my* bad behaviour all along, and he's a great guy for putting up with me. I guess that's very satisfying to him and has been reinforced thousands of times.

I end up by thinking to myself that he's sick and borderline insane. So by allowing his behaviour to pull me down, I'm just being stupid. I've told the boys hundreds of times that if they let him pull them down, he wins, they lose.

If it was relevant to my feelings toward him that I respect him, it would be torture for me to accept his behaviour. I guess in accepting that he has a personality disorder and there is nothing I can do about it, I'm able to distance myself from the craziness.

On November 16, my wonderful, dynamic mother died. After surgery to stabilize her spine, she'd remained alive for over a week, in great pain, and wishing to die.

I sat in my wheelchair by her hospital bed. At one point she managed to pull herself, by sheer willpower, over to the side of her bed so she could reach far enough to hug me. Something had eliminated her ability to talk, and all she could do was make stuttering noises. Her worst fear had always been losing her abil-ity to communicate.

The cervical collar she wore pressed into her back, making her cry and moan. When the nurses said there was nothing they could do about it, I lowered my mother's bed as much as I could and reached my hand under the collar. I could feel a ridge of hard foam digging into her. I asked the nurse if she could slice the foam off, but she said, "Sorry. You'll have to wait until Monday and ask the prosthetics guy if he can help you."

Once she left, I reached behind Mom, undid the Velcro straps that held the back piece in place and shaved the offending bump down smooth with my Leatherman knife. Mom and I somehow got the padding back in place, me reaching as far as I could from my wheelchair, using one hand to balance and stabilize me, Mom pulling herself to the edge of the hospital bed.

She couldn't eat, and they began to tube feed her, causing more pain and agony. But even though her body was wracked with pain, her eyes shone with love. True to her character, my mother gave me her strength and her power right to the very end of her life.

For a number of years before her death, Mom had been quite physically disabled. She had injured her back as a young woman, and for her entire life it plagued her. Surgery gone wrong when she was in her seventies made the situation worse. But despite the pain she suffered, her greatest joy was having family visit. Right up to the day she broke her neck, she was queen of the cribbage board. Sitting propped up by pillows in her armchair at the kitchen table, she'd have a twinkle in her eye as she skunked yet another opponent.

My father was devoted to her. They lived in a log house on the banks of a clear mountain stream. Dad had plenty of outside chores to keep him busy. But after Mom died, he began a rapid decline. Within eight months he went from cutting his own wood and maintaining his own house to being unable to look after himself.

That summer I went to Dad's place in Valemount and convinced him to come back to the farm with me. Once we found the right specialist, we learned he had damage to his lungs from having worked with asbestos as a young man. As he grieved my mother's passing, the lung damage took over with a vengeance.

I was grateful I could comfort him in his struggle, but there was nothing anyone could do to fix him. His lungs were destroyed, and he was too old for a transplant. Dad was on oxygen full-time. I gave him morphine through a line that health care nurses had taped onto his chest. Ativan calmed his distress when he couldn't breathe. I took his meals to his room for him and helped him to the bathroom across the hall. He would hold onto my wheelchair push bars and use them like he would a walker.

Dad's flame grew feebler and he became frailer every day. He was terrified to be left alone with Sandy. One time, when Dad was having a panic attack because he couldn't breathe, he rang the emergency bell I had set up for him. Sandy ran into Dad's room before I could get there. He flipped Dad over and began pounding on his back. Dad's ribs remained sore for the rest of his life.

When Dad reached a point where he was too weak for me to help him, he was transferred to the Grande Prairie Hospital. The day he died, I was sitting in the office of an oral surgeon in Edmonton, waiting for the completion of surgery to reshape Matti's jaw. His jaw had been broken on both sides in the car accident, and it had fused together improperly as he lay in a coma.

Matti and I left home on December 17 to travel the six hours to Edmonton in a blizzard for his surgery the next day. I knew my dad was dying, and I'd agonized over what to do: stay with my father or take my son for the time-sensitive surgery he was booked for? I thought, *What would Mom and Dad want me to do?* And I decided they would tell me to look after Mat. My brother came to stay with Dad, who was unconscious by this time.

Mat and I stayed in Edmonton a few more days for follow-up to his surgery, then returned to the farm. My brother and sister and I decided to wait until spring to hold Dad's memorial service in Valemount. That way his sister, my aunt Marjorie, could come from Saskatchewan, and people wouldn't have to travel in winter. We buried Dad's ashes on the family land, where my brother Gordie's ashes, my mother's ashes, and my nephew Jamie's ashes are also buried.

CHAPTER 10

I HAD MADE the decision after Matti's brain injury that I would do whatever it took to hold onto the farm for him. By 2006, two years after his accident, it was obvious his recovery had levelled off. He needed an afternoon nap and was in bed by nine o'clock every night. His attempts at returning to college failed, as did his attempts to shoe horses. He struggled to accomplish minor tasks. But he never gave up and, when allowed to work at his own pace, he could function and contribute on the farm. He was even starting to take a more active role in relation to his farm tasks.

My mind no longer skittered about with thoughts of getting away and starting a new life for myself. But life remained a see-saw. Sandy was vile and cruel during the day, then professed his love for me as we turned off the lights to go to sleep at night. I couldn't keep opening my heart, then getting kicked down for no reason. I thought that being in my own room, away from him, would help.

I got my friend and housekeeper, Corrine, to make up a bed for me with my electric blanket in the spare room. That night I was lying there reading when Sandy came charging through the doorway, red-faced and scowling. He blurted, "You get your ass back to your own bed. You're not pulling this bullshit on me."

"I'm so tired of your behaviour," I said. "I don't understand why you even want me in the same room with you, since you obviously detest me. Can't you tell me why you get so angry? Maybe if you explained what your problem is, I could help you."

He yelled, "You know what the doctor told you! You're the crazy one here! You need to go see a shrink!"

I knew it was pointless to argue. "I'm not going back into that room, so give it up."

Leaping from the doorway to the edge of my bed, Sandy grabbed the bed and started to flip it over. "You think you're so special! Well, you're nothing. You're a useless shit. That's what you are! You think you can control me! I'll show you what that gets you!"

With my paralyzed body, there was nothing I could do. If the bed went over, I would be under it to stay. I was sliding off, trying to hang onto the mattress to stop myself. I was terrified, but I did not want him to see my fear. I said, my voice calm, "If you don't stop, I will report you to the police first chance I get."

He slammed the bed down with a thud, then stormed off to his room, muttering.

Each night after that he taunted me from his room, muttering threats loud enough that I could hear them.

JOURNAL ENTRY: APRIL 8, 2008

Two days ago it came across the news that three children under the age of ten had been stabbed to death in a mobile home in Merritt, BC. The news report said the mother had gone to the corner store and, after arriving back home, came running out of her trailer, screaming and crying. Apparently the estranged father of the children, a roofer from Vancouver, had been spotted in Merritt about a week before. One neighbour was quoted as saying the father had expressed to him earlier how difficult it was to be separated from his family.

The story made the hair stand up on the back of my neck. It was pretty obvious what had happened. As usual, I said nothing aloud, but Sandy commented, "I'll bet the mother did it."

Of course all mothers are evil in his eyes. The whole thing brought back memories of the fear I lived with as a young mother, and the knowledge I still have that if I cross a certain line, he'll kill me.

This morning on the news, they reported that the father of the children had been in jail and there was a restraining order against him so he wouldn't bother the family. Since the murders, he'd been on the lam and was thought to be in Alberta, travelling with the family dog. Sandy's comment was, "The son of a bitch, why would he do that? I suppose they were fighting over the kids. He should have killed her. Why would he kill the kids? He should have just slit her throat."

It makes me feel nauseous to write this. This is by no means the first time he's made this type of remark. Pretty much every time there's a reported tragedy of a father slaughtering his family, Sandy makes a point of saying that the killer should have killed the mother, not the children. He's also said that he can understand how the father could do such a thing as slaughter his family if the mother pushed him too far. If she made him do it.

Journal entry: April 17, 2008

I believe it's getting to be time to find out what would happen if I reported Sandy for threatening me. He threatened tonight to push me down the elevator shaft, saying he'd probably hang but at least he'd have the satisfaction of killing me.

The craziness started because he was carrying on about Mat building a fence wrong. The usual: blaming me for all his problems with Mat, because Mat won't blindly listen to everything he says. He's definitely becoming crazier. He went and tore Mat's fence down with the tractor.

Sandy enjoys the people we attract. I think that's all that stops him from following through on his threats. That and the fact that I'm the money manager. He knows I do a good job of it, and he loves money. It would be hard to maintain his image if he murdered me. Pretty hard to explain pushing your paralyzed wife down the elevator shaft.

Journal entry: May 12, 2008

As Sandy was pushing himself into my face, with his crazy eyes blazing, spit flying, he was yelling "You think I'm scared of you? Huh? Huh? Well, I'm not... and you better be scared of me... You better be *very* scared of me... Everything here is *mine*... I've done everything... You've done nothing... I might hang but you won't get anything!"

During all the ranting about flipping my chair over or pushing me down the elevator shaft, he's in crazy mode, twitching, screaming, posturing in a very threatening manner. If I opened my mouth when he's raging, it would very likely pull the trigger.

He used to make me answer him all the time; I'd have to agree with all the crazy shit he was saying. The last few times I've refused to even answer. If it gets me a beating so be it.

◈

Before Mat's accident, he had bought a little Ford Taurus so he could keep his farrier tools in the trunk. He didn't want to take the chance of having them stolen from the back of the Ford Ranger he normally drove. The car got parked after Mat's accident. No one else had a reason to use it.

Sandy took the garbage to the dump one day, and when he returned he had someone with him, a seedy-looking guy about thirty-five years old. I was used to Sandy making friends everywhere he went, so I thought nothing of this fellow being with him. I watched them look over Mat's car, and Sandy then gave his new friend a grand tour of the barnyard area and shop. By the time they came over to the house, Sandy was bubbling with joy. "This is our new neighbour from across the road, Teddy. He's gonna come and work in the shop with me."

Ted had some sob story about being down on his luck and needing a car to get to work. Mat was easily influenced so— between Sandy and Ted—they talked him into giving up his little car. The deal was that Ted would pay it off in labour hours. I didn't trust Ted from the minute I met him, but Sandy was infatuated.

Ted became a fixture at our place. He helped Sandy in his shop almost every day, and they drove around the area together. Sandy went over to the house Ted was renting and helped him with some water problems. He loaned Ted tools and equipment. Ted was a big talker. He had all kinds of stories that were obviously fantasies about himself and his accomplishments. But I didn't care. I just stayed away from him.

Then one day Ted came to the house when I was alone. He managed to con forty dollars from me with the promise he'd pay it back in a day or two. A few days later he came along again, looking for more money. By this time I knew he was on the blacklist at both local convenience stores for not paying his bills. I had anticipated his second request, and I was ready with a question of my own.

"Hey, Ted. Any chance you could get me a pistol?"

Ted never missed a beat. He said, "No problem. I can get you a pistol, or I can make you a hand gun from a .22 long rifle."

"How much?"

"A couple hundred bucks for a cut-down gun would do it."

I said, "Okay. Well, if you come across one, grab it for me. But make sure you don't tell anyone I asked you to."

I had thought about getting a gun for a long time, but I hadn't known who to ask. Sandy had been rushing at me in attack mode lately, and after the bed-flipping incident, I wanted to have the ability to protect myself from him.

After I talked to Ted about the gun, though, I got scared. It gave me goosebumps to think I was actually considering it. I went through possible attack scenarios in my mind. I'll keep the gun in my wheelchair pouch in the daytime, I thought, and under my pillow, or the edge of my blankets, at night. If Sandy comes after me when I'm in bed, I'll grab it and warn him off. If he attacks me in the daytime, I'll quickly grab it from my wheelchair bag.

I lay in bed that night visualizing how it might play out. Sandy would come blasting through my door, screaming and ranting. I would grab the gun, point it at him, and calmly tell him, "Back off or I'll shoot you!"

But the more I thought about it, the more I realized what a ludicrous idea it was. When I'm lying flat, I have a hard time moving at all. And any fast movement causes me to go into a rigid spasm. I can only use one hand at a time; I need the other to balance and brace myself. He would be on top of me before I could even begin to get the gun out. If by pure luck I did reach it, the odds of stopping him with it were less than winning the lottery.

I was horrified to realize how crazy my idea was. Me pulling a gun on Sandy would no doubt mean signing my own death warrant. The way Sandy's behaviour was escalating, I knew something had to give. I just hoped it would be his heart when he was in a wild rage one day. I knew I couldn't use the gun even if Ted did get me one.

Jason had moved back to the farm after Mat's accident so he could help out as needed. He had gotten a job working for a local school board maintaining their IT systems, and he was living with his girlfriend downstairs at our house. A few days after I asked Ted about the gun, Jason's girlfriend saw someone at our fuel tank early one morning. She walked over in the pitch-dark to see who it was. It was Ted. He made up a story about losing his wallet and told her he thought he might have lost it in our yard. She was a naive young woman and took him at his word.

I waited for daylight to arrive, then went out on my power wheelchair, following Ted's tracks in the fresh skiff of snow. I could see that he had driven his old three-wheel Suzuki trike all around our equipment before arriving in the yard where the fuel tanks are. I could see footprints in the snow leading to the tanks. It didn't take a rocket scientist to figure out that Ted had first checked the gas tanks on our equipment. When he didn't score there, he headed into the yard to steal gas.

I never said anything about the gas theft. I knew Ted would deny it, plus I didn't want him to mention anything about the gun. A couple of days later, Ted came to the house while Sandy was out. He told me his father was dying back in BC and he had no money to get there. Could I possibly loan him a few hundred dollars?

I gave him two hundred dollars, and that was the last we ever saw of him.

CHAPTER 11

JOURNAL ENTRY: MARCH 30, 2009

Yesterday on the news there was a report about a man in the US who went into an old folks' home and shot ten people dead. He was trying to find his wife, who worked there and hid when she heard the commotion. This morning at the breakfast table Sandy said, "That guy in the States who shot all those old people was trying to kill his wife."

I said, "Uh huh."

Watching me with a twisted little smirk on his face, he said, "Well, he certainly can't be blamed for that. In fact, he deserves a medal. It's just too bad he killed all those other people and didn't even get his wife."

The lead-up to this morning's need to put me in my place was likely that, two days ago, Mike and Shauna Head phoned out of the blue and invited me to go for a tour in their helicopter. Of course I went, and it was fantastic, but I know Sandy's very bitter about it.

JOURNAL ENTRY: APRIL 10, 2009

It's usually just when things have escalated to extreme levels that I feel the need to write them down, but there's the "drip, drip," water-torture aspect to Sandy's behaviour as well. He threatens Mat steadily now, things like, "I'll burn your house down" or "I'll take the keys to your truck and hide them." (He never threatens Jay because he knows Jay could knock his block off.) He's also back to the habit he had when Mat was younger: smacking him in the head for any reason at all. Every therapist and doctor at the Glenrose has drilled into Mat the importance of protecting his head from any kind of blow. Sandy's aware of how important it is to protect Mat's damaged brain too. Jason's disgusted by his behaviour.

Pretty much every morning I receive a derogatory comment. I try to avoid making eye contact. But when I'm doing stuff in the kitchen, or eating, Sandy will sit and stare at me. He does it with Mat, too. It's creepy and bizarre.

It's odd how he always says I cut him to pieces with my tongue. I never criticize him and am very careful not to say anything negative. But he says my tongue hurts him far worse than his fists could ever hurt me. I wish I knew what he's hearing me say to him. Maybe it's voices in his head.

JOURNAL ENTRY: APRIL 24, 2009

It's an ongoing battle with Mat and Sandy about the general day-to-day operation of the farm. Mat does most of the calving-related chores and sometimes wants to make a few minor changes. I don't really see the benefits as being worth the effort on some things, but I tell myself that he's doing the work and it certainly won't hurt anything to try doing it his way. Sandy, on the other hand, completely freaks out when Mat makes a suggestion, starts calling Mat names, telling him how stupid he and all his ideas are, and forbids him to try anything. If someone else comes along with the exact same idea Mat had, quite often Sandy will be all over it. I know it really puzzles Mat when that happens and Sandy acts like Mat had never even brought it up.

They had an argument two days ago, lots of name-calling, which finally ended up with Sandy chasing Mat with a wrench or hammer or some such tool. Yesterday Mat was still upset and Sandy was all jolly. He always is after he throws a tantrum and gets his rage out. It leaves the rest of us with all his baggage.

Today, when Mat refused to be all chatty and jolly, Sandy threw a tantrum again, left the tractor, got in his car and drove away. Mat finished the feeding, which Sandy had been doing, and moved the windbreaks and calf shed to what he and I both deemed to be a more appropriate spot. When Sandy got home, he instantly found fault and said, "It won't work, blah blah blah, you stupid fucking idiot! Your mother must have put you up to that!"

For twenty minutes he threw cheap shots at both me and Mat, then was all sweet and lovable and expected us to follow his lead. I've come to the conclusion that he behaves very much like a drunk. Irrational, unpredictable, and mean. Only he doesn't need the alcohol to get him there. He went and moved the calf shelters back into the water run.

JOURNAL ENTRY: MAY 31, 2009

Mat, Jay, and I just finished a two-day workshop on self-empowerment and self-esteem. The focus of the workshop was on self-talk, assuming that you are putting yourself down, and on helping you to overcome negative thoughts about yourself. What we need is a workshop on how to deal with your spouse/father who's constantly belittling, attacking, and demeaning you.

Mat of course is the main target, because he has the most at stake. Mat's always working at something; he goes from daylight to dark. Often his sire disagrees with what he's doing. Actually, he *usually* disagrees. Then he orders Mat not to do whatever it is, in the way that Mat had planned, but to do it Sandy's way. Whether it's right or wrong.

He instantly puts Mat on the defensive by attacking and degrading him and his ideas. Mat either rolls over and caves, or he has to fight back. Sandy wants him to fight back so he can be justified in attacking him to begin with. When he can push Mat into reacting and getting angry, Sandy can say to himself and all his chums, when he tells them how ignorant Mat is, "See what I have to put up with. Is it any wonder I have to get so mad?"

That's one of his standard excuses for when he loses it and beats on me or Mat: "You shouldn't have made me mad. It's all your fault. If you didn't make me mad I wouldn't have to hit you!"

"Buggerlugs" is what he calls Mat. It's his name for any guy he looks down on.

❧

In October 2009, on an online dating site, Mat met a very pretty young nurse from Grande Prairie. Jenny Christensen had been athletic as a girl. She skied, skated, played ball, and excelled at competitive soccer. But teenage hormones wreaked havoc with her self-esteem, and she started to self-medicate by overeating. By the time she met Matthew, she had been struggling with being overweight for so long that she had nearly given up on life.

Matthew and Jenny clicked instantly, giving each other strength and support to overcome the difficulties they faced. As a nurse, Jenny was able to see beyond Matthew's obvious brain damage. She wasn't intimidated by it; in fact, she seemed intrigued by the challenge. By the springtime of 2010, Jenny had moved in with Mat, and his bachelor pad became a home.

Mat and Jenny planned a small wedding ceremony in their yard for August 22, 2010, with a Justice of the Peace to perform the rites and their closest friends in attendance. I watched early that morning as they set up chairs. My great-nephew Derrek put a stereo in place to play the music they had selected. Jenny's friends were in and out of the house, dressed as bridesmaids in matching mint-green gowns. Mat had asked three of his friends and his brother Jason to stand up with him, and they all wore casual western attire. Mat and Jenny had let the cat out of the bag that she was three months pregnant, and I was thrilled. They had already booked the Grovedale hall for a celebration party in October, and the entire community was invited to the dance.

I was so wrapped up in my happiness over the wedding that I hadn't registered Sandy's sour mood. The angry snarl that escaped his lips as we followed the trail to Mat and Jenny's yard startled me out of my dreamy little bubble.

"I wonder who he'll have over there?" Sandy growled. "If that fucking little creep is there, I'll kick his ass off the place. I'm fucking sick of putting up with Mat's shit around here."

I knew who Sandy meant: one of Mat's friends whom he disliked.

My stomach tightened as I listened to his ranting. Normally I didn't respond to his baiting, but I couldn't keep my mouth closed this time. "Why don't you grow up? Can't you ever be happy for Mat? Even on his wedding day?"

By this time we were within earshot of the yard full of people, so Sandy didn't answer. He sat down in one of the chairs the kids had set up. I rolled my power chair around the other side of the group, where I could keep an eye out for him causing any trouble, and began taking photos.

After the wedding ceremony, Sandy disappeared. I tried to find him, so that we could take a photo together with Jenny's parents and the newlyweds, but he was nowhere to be seen. When I finally got back to our house, Sandy was in his recliner watching TV. Nothing more was said about it. The only feeling I had about his behaviour at Mat's wedding was fatigue. I was so tired of being on constant alert, prepared to roll in between Sandy and whoever he was targeting, to prevent conflict.

The day after the wedding, Matthew and Jenny headed off on their honeymoon, taking along with them their two dogs, Tank and Bella, and my great-nephew Derrek, who had been working for us on the farm. They dropped Derrek off at his dad's place in Kamloops and continued on down to the coast.

While they were gone, I made plans to go to a weekend music festival my cousin Emilie and her family had been hosting for the past five years. Emilie had invited Laurie Wedler, who lived in our basement by this time, and me to do a working stock dog demonstration at the festival. Sandy didn't like Emilie, so to keep the peace I had never attended the festival, but this time I decided I was going, whether he was upset about it or not. I'd had enough of avoiding things I wanted to do just to keep from rocking the boat, and Laurie was on board for going with me.

The day of our departure grew closer, and one morning Sandy said, "Maybe I'll come with you guys."

I didn't want to go if that was the case. It would totally ruin the weekend. I knew he would just make things miserable for me. I thought fast. "Somebody has to stay home and look after the farm," I said. "We can't leave the sheep out at night, or the coyotes will eat them. Plus, Reg is supposed to come and pour concrete, remember? Someone needs to be home for that."

I was relieved when he grumbled, "Oh, sure. As usual, I have to do everything."

In the days that followed he didn't mention the festival again.

CHAPTER 12

MATTHEW AND JENNY got back from their honeymoon just after lunchtime on Thursday, September 2. Laurie and I had the Winnebago already loaded. We were ready to head for the Sweetwater festival. We were looking forward to working our dogs and to having a fun weekend together.

The newlyweds were glad to be home. Their trip had been a marathon driving excursion, spent visiting relatives along the way. They weren't too tired, though, to bring out the presents they had purchased for everyone. Laurie and I sat with them at the picnic table along the trail to admire the goodies.

The battered wooden picnic table sat in a shady little nook. I kept the spot nicely mowed all summer. One of my duties on the farm was keeping the grass mowed. I'd use an overhead sling lift to lift me onto my mower, which was entirely hand operated. Once I was on it, I was good to go.

Matthew and Jenny had planned to go to the festival with us but they were tired of travelling, and they told us they'd decided to stay home.

Their change of plans caught me off guard. Since Mat and Jenny were going to be with us, I'd figured I wouldn't have to worry about what was happening at home. Jason was planning to come to Sweetwater as well, so no one would be vulnerable to the crazier-than-normal mood Sandy had been in lately. Now, that wouldn't be the case.

Quickly I weighed the situation in my mind. I knew Reg was planning to come and pour concrete at the house, but we had everything ready to go for that, so that shouldn't be too stressful for Sandy. If Reg was here pouring concrete, I reasoned, that would also keep Sandy from getting too ramped up. I was always uneasy about leaving Matthew alone at the farm with Sandy. *But he won't be alone*, I reminded myself. *Jenny will be here.* I chastised myself for being such an overprotective mother.

Laurie and I loaded our four border collies in the Winnebago and headed out for the three-hour drive. I took the wheel, propped as usual in the driver's seat by four-inch foam chunks wedged between my body and the armrests, with an old wheelchair cushion behind me and a footstool for my feet. The unit was rigged with hand controls, so as long as I was wedged firmly in place and couldn't tip sideways, I was fine.

We hadn't reached the main road yet when we saw Jason turn off the highway, headed up the long driveway toward us. With his red hair and brown eyes, Jason's colouring was different from his father's, but he had the same sharp intelligence and powerful physique. He was capable of handling any task presented to him, from farm work to computer network maintenance. We waved and kept going until I looked in my rearview mirror and saw Jason backing up his truck to catch up with us. I stopped, and when he caught up with us he jumped out of his truck. I heard a door slam, and I realized that the door to my wheelchair lift must have come open. Luckily, Jason had flagged us down.

Jason jogged up alongside of the motorhome and opened the regular entry door. "So, you guys are off to the festival, huh?"

"Yep. Are you still coming?"

"Yes. Mat said I could borrow his holiday trailer, so I'm on my way down to check it out now. Christina is arriving from Edmonton tomorrow, and we'll head to Sweetwater when she gets here."

"Great. It should be fun. Mat and Jenny have decided to stay at the farm, though. They're exhausted from all that travelling."

"Maybe they'll change their minds tomorrow," Jason said. "They could stay in the motorhome with you if they do, couldn't they?"

"Oh, for sure. We have lots of room. Right, Laurie?"

Laurie nodded.

It made my heart swell to see Jason so happy and carefree. I was glad he'd be taking a break and coming to the festival with us. His job with the school board could be stressful. He'd built a new house with his previous girlfriend in 2007, but within a year they had separated, leaving Jason alone in the big empty place. He was finally getting his life back on track. I couldn't wait to meet his new girlfriend, Christina Hopkins, whom he had had his first date with six months before, when he went to Edmonton to get his passport renewed.

After travelling for about an hour, Laurie and I stopped for a burger in a little town called Beaverlodge. While she ran in to get the food, I transferred onto my wheelchair and rolled back to the accessible bathroom in the RV. Using my sliding board, I transferred onto the toilet and used a catheter to empty my bladder.

My education into how the urinary system functions had begun after my accident when I was informed by nurses in the ICU at Edmonton's University Hospital that for the rest of my life I would have to use a catheter to void my bladder. When you have a spinal cord injury, even though you no longer have control of your bowels or bladder, they still have to function. It was a huge shock for me to learn that little fact of life.

When the reality first sank in for me that I was trapped in a strange new body, it shattered my identity. I hated my weakness and felt that my body had betrayed me. But I learned very quickly to be grateful for what I could do, and I'd gotten better and better at adapting.

Laurie and I devoured our meal, then headed on down the road. We made a grand entrance when we finally pulled into the farmyard at Rolla, where the Sweetwater 905 Art and Music Festival is held. My dog, Glen, climbed up on the dash in his excitement, eliciting grins from the people milling around everywhere.

As we rolled into the Mattson's yard, we passed a machine shop, then four wooden grain bins, that had been made into mini art studios for the festival. A ninety-degree angle took us swinging to the right, where there were more small outbuildings and a hip-roof barn, all of which had been converted to studios and display spaces for the festival.

Across from the barn was my cousin Emilie's own studio, along with her yard and house. Everything was decked out with artwork and beautifully landscaped. Across the creek to the south, I saw a large stage surrounded by concession and holiday trailers. Perched on top of an old log building with a sign that said "Beer Gardens" was a scaled-down wooden Viking ship, complete with bedraggled-looking sails. People ranging in age from toddlers to grey-haired seniors were strolling about.

My father and Emilie's father were brothers, and I've idolized her since I was a child. She is a natural horsewoman and a talented dog trainer, as well as being an amazing artist. Emilie can do anything she sets her mind to. Her artwork is anything but traditional western art, and her material of choice for quite some time in creating her sculptures was cow placenta. Some people love her work and some people hate it, but everyone notices it.

Emilie herself is a work of art. She's in her sixties now, with more energy than most twenty-year-olds. She's a little over five feet tall and around a hundred and ten pounds, solid and fit with wild, wild hair. Larry, Emilie's husband, is the quintessential rancher. He loves the farm and his cows. For Larry, getting out consists of going to the local coffee shop or auction mart.

Larry came to direct us to the place he and Emilie figured would be best for us. Laurie had taken over the driving by now, and she backed the motorhome into a tight spot between the back of a little bunkhouse and a fenced paddock. Laurie was delighted to see there was an outhouse right handy. When I told Larry that I would need power for my electric blanket, he said in his slow drawl, "That won't be a problem. I'll go find you a cord."

Another of the learning curves I experienced with my spinal cord injury was getting used to my body's dysfunctional thermostat. My body stays at the temperature of my surroundings, and I can't stand the cold at all. I've always got a blanket or a custom made zip-up snuggly bag wrapped around my legs; my sister Bobbi and my friend Shirley Strid make them for me. I usually have a hot pack or a heated wheat bag down by my feet inside the snuggly too, to keep the chill off my lower body.

Laurie and Larry levelled the motorhome with blocks and pulled the awning out. They set up the portable kennels for the dogs beneath that. The dogs were excited. They knew we were there to work sheep. Our location wasn't perfect though, because the sheep were in the outdoor arena right next to where we parked, and the dogs could see them standing there.

Keeping a border collie confined or tied up within eyesight of sheep isn't a good thing. The dog will lie there and stare at the sheep, trying to control them with his eyes. It's unnerving for the sheep. When the sheep in the outdoor arena saw our dogs, they clustered together and stared back, looking like a huge ball of wool with bug eyes attached. We decided we'd cover the dog kennels with blankets once we got settled in.

Once we had the Winnebago all set for night, with my electric blanket plugged in and warming my bed, we decided to take the dogs for a walk and have a look around the place. When I travel to dog competitions I bring my power wheelchair and a little manual wheelchair for use in the motorhome. The power chair is often dirty from rolling through sheep manure and mud, so I don't like to use it inside.

Laurie had already unloaded my power chair from the back of the Winnebago with the wheelchair lift. I brought the lift back up, got onto it on my manual chair, took the lift down and rolled my manual chair out onto the grass. I arranged my snuggly bag on the seat of my power chair, then placed my transfer board between the two chairs and slid across to my power chair. After making sure my legs were tucked in correctly, I threw a heat pack down by my feet, zipped up the snuggly, put my jacket on, clipped the arm rest onto my wheelchair, and was ready to go for a walk.

I let Glen and Zeke out and commanded them to come with me. They did, though I could tell all they could think of was getting over to where the sheep were. Zeke was eight years old, in his prime and very, very tough. I had to keep complete control of him or he would do whatever it took to make a sheep obey him. He's a traditional border collie with a coat of long, shiny black hair, white socks, a white speckled muzzle, and a white collar. One look at him, and you know he's the alpha dog. Sheep sense that right away and rarely argue with him.

My other dog, Glen, is a comedian. He's got short hair that's mottled black and white; a little girl once called him a Dalmatian. Half of Glen's face is white, with a brown eye on that side. The other half is black, with a blue eye. His charac-ter completely matches his looks. When he's working he's totally serious, but otherwise he's goofy and lovable, easily intimidated, but good-natured and never looking for trouble. Glen is more likely to shoulder-check a sheep to redirect it than he is to bite, or "grip," it. Zeke doesn't hesitate to bite if he thinks he can get away with it.

Laurie fetched her dogs, Splash and Call, and we headed off to look around. I was hoping we'd find a bit of room for the dogs to run. We tried to go out through a paddock, only to discover a muddy little water run that was impassable for my wheelchair. There were people all about, and the dogs were distracted. They wouldn't relax enough to empty their bowels and bladders. We tried a different route, through an old hay yard. That was better, but I couldn't go very far because of the rough terrain. My dogs got a bit shortchanged on exercise, although they did empty out.

Once we'd returned the dogs to their kennels, Laurie and I continued around the art displays. I was proud of the quality of the work I was seeing, proud for Emilie and for all the other artists putting on the show. The atmosphere was electric, with everybody getting geared up for the next day.

Around nine o'clock Laurie and I settled the dogs in their kennels and fed them, then got ready for bed. Everything was going great, and I was looking forward to tomorrow.

CHAPTER 13

FRIDAY MORNING DAWNED clear and sunny. Laurie volunteered to take the dogs for a walk while I made coffee and fixed us each a bowl of cereal with yogurt. I pondered the question of whether I should put in an indwelling catheter, which would keep my bladder drained into a leg bag, or gamble on being able to get from wherever I was to the facilities in the motorhome.

My body is high maintenance, like the proverbial hothouse plant. It demands strict adherence to a meticulous routine, and any deviation from that can prove disastrous. If I can't empty my bladder promptly at the required time, it's always going to be a bad scene. A condition called autonomic dysreflexia (AD) can cause my blood pressure to soar and make me pass out until the pressure is relieved. I carry an emergency medical card in my wallet in case of such an event. Anything from a full bladder to a foot crushed in the door to a pressure sore somewhere can be a trigger for AD. The other possibility when my bladder overfills is that it will simply release, anytime and anyplace. That creates an entirely different set of complications.

For each new situation, intermittent versus indwelling was a huge decision to make. Indwelling catheters promote bladder infection so they aren't optimum for your health. I decided to opt for intermittent catheterizing that day, which meant I'd have to time things carefully.

The stock dog demo Laurie and I were conducting was booked for two o'clock. Emilie had borrowed a small flock of ewes from the local Hutterites. I wasn't sure if the sheep had ever been worked by dogs before. Often, sheep who haven't will charge at a dog and refuse to be herded. The dog has to get aggressive to teach them who's boss. It's not a good thing in a demo for a dog to bite a sheep, so to make sure this flock would be controllable, Laurie and I decided to work them a bit first.

Just before eleven British Columbia time, noon in Alberta, we headed over to the small outdoor arena where the sheep were. The plan was that we'd work the sheep a bit, do some visiting, and then I'd go empty my bladder before the demo. Everything was timed to the minute.

The main trail leading into the arena had a little gate made from a rusted antique metal wagon wheel with hinges welded on. I untied the rope halter shank that held it closed, only to realize I couldn't get my wheelchair through a mud puddle.

Emilie had walked up behind me. "Uh oh, the kids must have let the water tank overflow last night when they watered the horses," she apologized.

She pointed out a tractor-sized gate halfway down the south side of the arena fence. If I went through a series of smaller gates behind the bunkhouse, she explained, I could reach the tractor gate and enter the arena that way. When I got there though, the big gate was too heavy for me to open. Laurie saw me struggling and she came around to open it for me. I went through, Zeke and Glen at my side. I rolled out to the middle of the arena and told my dogs to lie down. They did, even though they were ready to explode with wanting to work so badly. The sheep clustered against the far fence, staring at my dogs and trying to be invisible. The stronger ewes pushed the weaker ones to the outside edge.

We were ready to get started. Sitting there in my chair, soaking up energy from the brilliant northern British Columbia midday sun, I felt blessed. I knew I'd always hate being tied to a wheelchair, but I was grateful to have such amazing friends and top-of-the-line dogs. I figured I was a lucky woman.

As I watched the ewes jostle about, I visualized the course I would send the sheep through. I'd tie Glen to the fence and work Zeke first. He gets so nervous if he has to wait. As I was plotting out my strategy, from the corner of my eye I saw Larry come over to the fence and hand a cordless phone to Laurie. She took it from him and headed out toward me. I cautioned my dogs to stay where they were, resenting the intrusion.

Laurie handed me the phone.

"Hello?" I said.

Mat's voice came on the line. He said calmly, "I'm sorry to ruin your holiday, but I just shot your husband."

I was focussing my attention on Glen and Zeke so they wouldn't take off after the sheep. I knew the minute they heard my voice they'd be ready to spring into action. To hear Matthew talk like that, even as a joke, shook me.

I replied curtly. "Mat! I don't have time for fooling around right now. Be serious. What do you want?"

"Mom. I'm not joking. I shot Dad."

The tone of his voice convinced me it was true. A vice squeezed my head. "Oh my God, Matti. Where is he?"

"He's at my shop."

The pressure in my head intensified. I pictured Sandy lying injured in Matthew's shop. "How badly is he hurt?"

"He's dead."

This could not be happening. "Are you sure?"

"Yes."

All the strength drained from my body. I slumped in my wheelchair. My right arm, propped on the armrest, held up the massive weight of my head.

I heard Mat speaking as if from a great distance.

"I phoned 911."

"Are you okay? You're not hurt? Where are you?"

"I'm okay. I'm at home waiting for the police."

"All right. I'll be home as soon as I can get there."

Disconnecting from Matthew's call, I took a few deep breaths to calm my racing mind. Then I dialed Jason. He picked up on the second ring.

"Jay, you have to get home right away. Matti just called me. He said he shot your father!"

"What?"

"I don't think he was joking."

"I'm on my way."

When I ordered my dogs to come with me, they were puzzled. They tried to defy me by going toward the sheep. I knew no one else would be able to call them off, so I took the time to control them. With Glen and Zeke beside me, I took the phone over to where Larry was standing at the fence, handed it to him, and said to him and Laurie, "Matti just shot Sandy. I have to get home."

"What?"

"Yes. He said he's dead. I have to get home. I need a ride. Can you give me a ride, Larry?"

My mind alternated between going a hundred miles an hour, like a recording on fast forward, and feeling like a frozen block, completely blank.

At least Matti's safe, I thought. *Sandy can't hurt him if he's dead.* I had no clue how terrifying for all of us the road ahead would be.

Zeke and Glen stood stock still, vibrating with nerves as they stared at the sheep. I had to get stern with them to make them follow me. Back at our parking spot, I put the dogs into their kennels, transferred onto my manual wheelchair and took the lift up into the motorhome. I knew I had to get an indwelling catheter put in. Who knew when or where I'd be able to empty my bladder. My hands trembled as I struggled to insert it.

Emilie showed up just as I was finished. "What's going on?" she asked.

I said, "Matti shot Sandy. He's dead."

"I'll grab my purse and drive you back there."

"No," I told her. "You have to stay and look after your festival. Larry said he would take me."

Laurie arrived to ask if she should pack up the Winnebago and head for home. "I'm sure there's nothing you can do to help Matti right now," I told her. "You may as well stay and do the demo for Emilie."

This can't possibly be happening, I thought. *Please let it be some crazy nightmare.* I was deadly calm one second, the next second shaking like a leaf.

I could hear Larry outside. He called up that he had his truck gassed up and was ready to go.

"I'll be right down," I called back. "I need a snack bag," I said to Emilie. "Could you please get me one?"

Still in shock, I'd resorted to my usual planning when getting ready for a road trip. Laurie and Emilie tossed a bottle of water and some chips and granola bars from the motorhome kitchen into a white plastic bag for me.

I rode down on the lift. Emilie grabbed the handgrips on the back of my wheelchair and pushed me over to Larry's truck. Laurie, walking beside me, said suddenly, "You don't have your leg blanket. You're always frozen. I'll go grab it for you!"

"No, that's okay. I'll be fine without one," I said.

Larry carried me over to the passenger seat of his little truck, then loaded my wheelchair into the back.

As we drove, Larry and I talked non-stop. We talked about dog training and about the rate of alcohol consumption at the festival. We chatted to fill the air, trying to act like everything was normal. My mind was in turmoil, but on the outside I remained calm.

Silently, I went over all the red flags I'd been seeing in Sandy's behaviour over the summer. I agonized over the premonitions I'd had about leaving for the weekend. I knew what had happened wasn't my fault, but I also knew it wouldn't have happened if I'd been home.

There was no doubt in my mind that Sandy had instigated something. My brain screamed at me: *Sandy pushed Matti over the edge. He did something horrible. What was he doing in Matti's shop? Did he attack Matti there? Matti's life is done. Jason will be destroyed. We're all done now. I'm so tired of life being so damn hard.*

Larry and I had just driven through Beaverlodge when my cellphone rang. It was someone from the RCMP in Grande Prairie. When I told her where we were, she asked if we'd turn around and go back to the detachment in Beaverlodge. Officers there would drive me to Grande Prairie.

When we reached the Beaverlodge detachment, Larry unloaded my wheelchair, lifted me onto it, handed me the bag of snacks, and wheeled me around to the front of the building. Two officers came out the front door. The older one said he'd been informed my husband had been shot and was possibly deceased. I told him I'd heard the same thing. The officers seemed puzzled by my calm demeanour, as if they'd expected a more emotional reaction from me.

The younger officer said he would drive me to Grande Prairie. I handed Larry my snack bag to hold while the constable lifted me into the passenger seat of an RCMP truck, then loaded my wheelchair in the back. Larry gave me a hug before turning away with tears in his eyes. Although I was neither hungry nor thirsty, I clung to my snack bag desperately. I didn't want to let it out of my sight. That bag and the cellphone I was clutching were the only things I had any control over. Now, with Larry gone, I felt utterly helpless and at the mercy of strangers.

The constable behind the wheel appeared to be about Matthew's age. We didn't talk much on the way to Grande Prairie, though I told him that Mat and Jenny had just come back from their honeymoon the day before. It never occurred to me that the cops might be trying to set things up for me to make incriminating statements about Matti.

As we drove, I thought back to a conversation Matti and I had had two weeks earlier, just before his wedding. "Is there any chance we can get Dad committed to an insane asylum?" he'd asked me.

I'd told him, "No, Mat. It doesn't work like that. You can't just call the police and have someone picked up and locked away. It would only make your father worse, because the police would stir things up and then go away thinking he's a great guy and we're the problem. Besides, he doesn't think he's wrong in his actions. So is he wrong? Like, if you don't believe you're wrong, then are you?"

Mat thought for a while, then said, "Well, what does society say?"

I realized then that I was trying to justify Sandy's behaviour, as I'd been doing for nearly three decades.

"You're right," I answered Mat. "Society says he's wrong, and he knows it. He wouldn't act the way he does in front of anyone but us."

My cellphone rang. It was Matti, by this time in custody at the RCMP detachment in Grande Prairie. "I guess I need to have a lawyer. Who should I call?"

I instantly thought of Darryl Carter, who had always performed any legal work we needed done. Darryl's number was in my address book, which was in the bag attached to my wheelchair. Not thinking clearly, I told Mat to call me back in a half hour or so.

The constable parked alongside the curb when we arrived at the Grande Prairie detachment. I was in a fog, only vaguely aware of him lifting my chair from the back of the truck, setting it on the sidewalk, and then pushing it up beside the passenger door. As I opened the truck door, a bottle of water slipped from the bag I held on my lap. I watched as it tumbled in slow motion through the air, thudded off the side step of the truck, flipped onto its side, and landed with a splash in a deep puddle next to the curb. I was acutely aware of the smell of fresh rain. I heard children laughing at the nearby courthouse water fountain. People walked past on the sidewalk, talking. Birds sang in the hedge along the street.

The spell was broken when Constable Kirschner lifted me out of the truck. After he had seated me in my wheelchair, I headed for the ramp leading into the building. He called out for me to wait for him. By now, the reality was sinking in. If I hadn't been in a wheelchair, I would have been running as fast as I could. All I could think of was getting to where Matthew was. I was moving so fast in my chair that the young constable had to jog to keep up with me.

Inside the building, Jenny and her mom and dad were sitting in chairs lined up along the wall. They had stunned looks on their faces. Jenny's four-year-old niece was sitting on her Poppa's knee, looking near to tears. "Would you mind coming with me, please?" the young constable said to me. "I'd like to ask you a few questions."

When a police officer says that, you don't reply, "Yes, I would mind." You just agree and go along. At least that's what you do until you learn the ropes. This was all new to me, so I followed the young officer down the hall.

CHAPTER 14

ONCE YOU'VE BEEN through the process of dealing with police, you learn that you do not have to talk to them without a lawyer present. You can refuse. Not that it made any difference in the end. It was probably a good thing that Mat and Jason and I all told our stories and got it over with, because we told nothing but the truth. It's just that we were naive. We didn't know it's not uncommon for your words to be twisted and used later in a completely different context.

In my ignorance, I didn't realize the cops would be biased toward imposing the most serious charge they could. For some reason, I expected they would be neutral. That they would wait until they'd taken a look at the big picture before making judgment calls. I guess it's understandable that cops sometimes jump to conclusions. However, in this case, I was certain that once they understood our family dynamics, we'd be able to rationally sort out what had happened.

Even though I had no idea how the shooting had taken place, I knew without question that Mat had not instigated whatever led up to it. The police needed to understand that Sandy was the violent one. He was the one who was capable of committing murder. Mat was the least violent person I knew. Whatever had caused him to shoot his father, there had to be some sort of extreme provocation. The shock I felt at Sandy's death had not yet given way to the nightmarish terror I would feel every minute of the day for months to come.

As the young constable was hustling me through a door toward the interrogation room, I asked if he'd get me a phone book so I could find a lawyer for Matti. I had my cellphone with me and had tried to get hold of Darryl Carter, but he wasn't in his office. It was the Friday before the Labour Day weekend, and many people were already gone for the holiday. I searched the phone book to see who else I could call when my cellphone rang.

It was Brian Lofstrom, who told me that he'd called Roy Carter, Darryl's brother, and that Roy was already at the police station. The last time I'd seen Roy was a few months earlier out at the Lofstrom farm, at the wedding of his son, Jarin, to Amber Lofstrom. I never thought of Roy as a lawyer, since I hadn't been associated with him in that context. Our friendship had begun three decades earlier when I was a jockey and Roy's family was involved with horse racing. Our paths continued to cross since I was a fan of Jarin's chuckwagon racing team, and Jarin and I shared an interest in training border collies. I was hugely relieved to learn Roy was at the detachment. When I tried to call him I couldn't get through, but I was comforted to know he was nearby.

I'd learn later that, as members of the Grovedale Volunteer Fire Department, Brian and Sherry had been notified by pager of Mat's 911 call. Shocked and alarmed, they had rushed toward our farm, arriving at the turnoff before the RCMP did. Brian wanted to continue on to the farm, to be there with Matti until the police arrived, but Sherry reminded him they were required to wait at the road until instructed otherwise by the RCMP. It was the official duty of the volunteer fire department to stage at the entry to the residence in question, and nothing more. So Brian and Sherry did the only thing they could think of to help Mat. They phoned Roy Carter.

When Roy got the call from Brian, he was on his way home to his farm. He wheeled his truck around instantly and headed back toward Grande Prairie. Much later, he would tell me that as he was driving, his mind spun back nearly thirty years to a similar situation. A friend and classmate of his from college, an intelligent and accomplished young man poised for a lifetime of contribution to society, had killed his violent and abusive father.

Roy didn't have the experience, wisdom, or means at the time to aid his friend. He watched helplessly as the young man's life spiralled downward. His friend served a prison sentence, then, upon his release, wound up living as a street person. It was something Roy never got over. When he heard what had happened with Matti, it was like déjà vu. Only this time Roy wasn't a naive, powerless college lad. He knew instantly how dire the situation was. He knew we were facing nearly insurmountable odds in our quest to save Mat's life from complete destruction. He'd seen it all before.

I'd also learn later that while I was trying to reach Roy by phone, he was looking for me. He'd asked the cops at the detachment where I was, and they'd said I was talking to Victim Services. They told Roy they would let me know right away that he wanted to see me, which they didn't do.

In the interrogation room, the young constable informed me that I didn't have to talk to him. He would like to hear my thoughts on what might have happened, though, he said. The police were trying to understand what could have caused Matti to shoot his father. In retrospect, I wished I had told him I had no idea what happened and left it at that, because I truly didn't. Instead, I chattered on for an hour and a half about what I imagined might have taken place.

I learned afterwards that while I was being questioned in one room, Jason was in a nearby room being interrogated. He, like me, was in a state of shock, and he rattled on without realizing he could be telling the police something they would use against Mat. Jay and I both knew that regardless of what Mat had done, there was no way he planned or instigated it, because his brain does not work that way. We didn't grasp that anyone would try to paint him as the villain.

When I came out of the small windowless room after my interrogation, I spotted Jason and Roy right away. Roy asked the RCMP to find us a room where we could have some privacy. They pointed to a private office, and Roy waited outside while Jason and I went in together. We were both crying as Jason leaned over, hugging me as I sat in my wheelchair. After a couple of minutes we pulled it together and called Roy in. Wiping away our tears, we were both suddenly fiercely angry with Sandy. Even though neither of us knew the full story, we knew without a doubt that Mat had not instigated anything.

Roy had already contacted Dave Cunningham, a well-known criminal lawyer, he said, and Dave had agreed to represent Mat.

After the three of us had consulted for a few minutes, we went back into the hall. Someone from Victim Services approached us, offering support. I took a card, saying we would call them. Roy later advised me, however, that Victim Services would be working on the assumption Mat was in the wrong, and it would be best to leave them out of things.

Jenny and Judy were still sitting in the waiting area when we got there. After hugging them for a while, we went up to the desk to ask if we could see Mat. They wouldn't let us, and Roy said we might as well go home; he would look after Mat for us.

Jenny's dad, Denis, had taken her little niece home by this time, but Judy's truck was parked outside. Jay lifted me onto the front seat, threw my wheelchair in the back, and the four of us headed out to the farm.

CHAPTER 15

Statement Of: Jason Crichton 2010-1080663
Conducted In: Grande Prairie, Alberta
Conducted By: Constable D.L. Maile
Taken On: September 3, 2010 @ 2:38 p.m.
DLM: Denotes Constable D.L. Maile
JC: Denotes Jason Crichton

DLM: Jason, how do you say your last name?

JC: Crichton.

DLM: It is Crichton. Okay, like the author.

JC: Same.

DLM: Right on. Okay, one of my favourites. Ah, it's 2:38 and it is...

JC: Is it really?

DLM: Yeah, 2:38 in the afternoon, September, it's Friday, September 2nd, or September 3rd.

JC: Correct, yes.

DLM: Okay.

JC: I gave up my watch earlier, 'cause the cuffs were digging into it.

DLM: Okay, we'll get that back to you and your phone as well... I guess a series of unfortunate incidents has occurred that brought you here today, and I—my condolences. I'm sorry, and I guess what I want to talk to you about is what's going on. Like, can you tell me, from your perspective, what you know?

JC: What happened?

DLM: Yeah.

JC: I was at my office… and I was actually just starting to eat lunch when I received a phone call from my mother, who was noticeably upset. She told me that my brother had just phoned her and said that he had shot my father. And she said she was fairly certain he wasn't joking. At which point I told her I was on my way home. I left the office. Told them I have to go deal with something. And drove out to the farm…

On my way out I phoned my brother, on my way out of town. Saying, "What did you do?" And he told me. And I told him, he needs to put it down, if he's still holding it. And he needs to go somewhere out in the open and call 911. At which point he told me he had. And he had told them he had shot him. And that the police said they were on their way. I drove past your group of police staging on my way home, and phoned him again. And said, "You need to make sure you are out in the open somewhere." I wasn't certain how, what they knew. And I didn't want him to, you know, come walking out of somewhere and get himself into even deeper trouble. At which point I pulled up and he was sitting at a picnic table. And I sat down with him and said, "We're gonna wait here until the police show up." And then I believe a corporal phoned and spoke with Mat. And then he asked to speak with me. And told, asked me, to drive him down the road to meet them. And then he and Mat spoke for a few minutes more. And I went over and checked my father. Just to verify. And then we got into my truck and drove out about a hundred yards past the property line. A vehicle, likely the K-9 vehicle, stopped us and ordered us to get out. And then we got out and we were both handcuffed. And I was asked some questions and put in the back of a police car.

DLM: Okay, so he called you, what phone did he call you from?

JC: My mother called me.

DLM: Oh, I'm sorry, your mother called you. What phone did she call you from?

JC: She called me from my cousin's phone, because there is no cell service in Rolla.

DLM: Do you remember specifically what the conversation was?

JC: I answered the phone and said, "what's up?" She said, "Your brother just phoned and said he shot your father. I don't think he's joking."

DLM: And then what did you say?

JC: I said, "He said what?" Or "he did what?" That was my statement. And she said, "I don't think he was joking." And I said, "Okay, I'm on my way."

DLM: Just a short conversation?

JC: Yeah, I hung up and went out the door.

DLM: Okay.

JC: 'Cause she said she was getting in a vehicle, someone was gonna drive her. She's paralyzed from here down.

DLM: Okay, so you got this phone call from your mom.

JC: Yes.

DLM: And it was a brief conversation. You right away leave work, hop in your vehicle.

JC: I phoned him. Said, my initial conversation, my opening words were, "What did you do?" And he's like, "I shot him."

DLM: That's it.

JC: Like, "I shot him and he's dead." And I said, "You have to get out somewhere away from everything. You know, so that you're not gonna look like you're hiding anything. And you need to phone 911." And he said he already had. And I said, "Okay, I'm on my way out there and I'll be there shortly." I said, "You need to make sure you are out somewhere." I told him to go sit at the picnic table by his house, 'cause it's out in the open. There is nothing around. Because I wasn't—I saw like nine cop cars. I wasn't entirely certain they weren't gonna be very assertive, I guess would be the word. When they went in. And I wanted to make sure he wasn't standing somewhere where it looked like he might try something, or anything. And then I hung up and I kept driving.

DLM: And did he say okay, or…?

JC: He said, "Yeah, that's fine."

DLM: How did he seem?

JC: Calm… And then when I got there and got out of the truck, I sat down and talked to him for a couple of minutes.

DLM: Was there anyone else on the whole property at all?

JC: As far as I know, no.

DLM: Okay, so you didn't see anyone.

JC: I saw no one else. I saw no trace of anyone else.

DLM: Okay.

JC: Other than my father.

DLM: And, I know this is hard, but where was he?

JC: He was lying by the east door of my brother's shop.

DLM: Okay.

JC: Face down.

DLM: Okay, and how far is that from the picnic table?

JC: 75 metres.

DLM: Okay. You knew it was him for sure.

JC: There was no question.

DLM: Okay.

JC: While my brother started talking to the police, I told him, "I'm gonna go over." And I wandered over and looked and checked for a pulse. And, you know, looked underneath. I didn't move him, I just stepped over. Felt his wrist, looked. And I could see blood pooling out of his mouth. And there was no pulse. And he was a distinctly unhealthy shade of purple.

DLM: Okay. So, go on to your conversation. What exactly was said?

JC: I asked him what happened. And I'm vaguely paraphrasing, because I wasn't, this was secondary. I was trying to just make sure everything was in one piece, kind of thing. Um, they had been working. And my father is not, or was not, the most rational person in the world. My brother told me that my father decided to throw a fit at my brother and was trying to run him over with the tractor. Which isn't entirely unbelievable. It's happened before. And so my brother went to his shop and started unloading, opening the gun safe. And by the time my father got there, my brother had loaded three bullets into his .22 pistol. And my brother said he was going to shoot my father, and then I—he didn't really explain what my father did. And then he shot him.

DLM: Okay.

JC: And then he put the gun away and called the police. At which point the RCMP phoned.

DLM: Okay. Did he get any more specific than that?

JC: Not really, no.

DLM: So he told you just, just so I understand, that they were working in the shop.

JC: Ah, they weren't working in the shop. They were working—he was in a bobcat, my father was in a tractor.

DLM: Okay, so they were doing yard work.

JC: Yard work, yeah.

DLM: Okay. What exactly were they doing, do you know?

JC: Clearing. My mother has been planning to pour a concrete pad at their place, at my parents' house. They've cleared a bunch of dirt out of there. And my brother was moving it to do something. I didn't get details on what, and I don't know what my father was doing in the tractor. All I know is that they began to fight. And apparently my father decided to chase after my brother with a tractor. Which is probably true. And then my brother got to his shop and went inside. And then my father followed him in.

DLM: Did he say this occurred over on your brother's side?

JC: I think it started over on my parents' side. And then my brother went to his side, and my father followed him.

DLM: In the tractor?

JC: I'm not sure about that, I don't think so. I think he walked, because I didn't see the tractor. It didn't register anyway in the area. I don't remember seeing the tractor in the area.

DLM: Did he say why they were fighting, what it was about?

JC: It's really hard to say. My dad is the type to just start a fight because he can... So it could have been anything. From my brother wasn't spreading the dirt properly to he didn't want my brother to spread the dirt at that exact moment in time.

DLM: Right.

JC: It was more likely than not him just pushing buttons.

DLM: Okay, okay, this is your assumption on your part, but...

JC: Most likely. This is history.

DLM: Yeah, experience.

JC: This is based on past history. I've experienced the same basic things.

DLM: Okay.

JC: When my brother says this, I don't doubt it.

DLM: Yeah, okay. Alright. So, and then your brother says, he went to his shop, and this is where his gun is, or guns are?

JC: Yes.

DLM: Plural or single?

JC: Plural, but I don't know how many. I know he has a small barrel 410 shotgun and a .22 pistol.

DLM: Okay.

JC: I don't know if he has anything else in there. At one point he had a rifle, but it was a really big one and it hurt his shoulder to shoot, and I think he may have sold that.

DLM: Okay.

JC: I've never looked into it, because the last time I talked to him he couldn't remember the combination.

DLM: Okay.

JC: But I think he—when I last saw him at the farm, he had it written on his hand.

DLM: The combination for his locks, or gun safe?

JC: Yeah.

DLM: But it's in his shop.

JC: It's in his shop.

DLM: It's not in the house.

JC: No.

DLM: Does he keep any guns in the house?

JC: No.

DLM: Okay. So he tells you that they got into a fight. What made him decide to go get his gun?

JC: I don't think it was an entirely just spur-of-the-moment thing. Like, my brother has come close a couple times in the past. My father has been very—the term "manipulative abusive bastard" is probably the most appropriate term for him. And he's pushed my brother very, very far before. So I wouldn't be entirely surprised if my brother has thought about this a few times.

DLM: Right.

JC: But generally, the whole premise is, just don't do it. You know, like, if he's making you that angry, just leave.

DLM: But essentially, he says he went and got his gun loaded. Three bullets, he told you.

JC: Yeah, he was very specific. He had three bullets in the gun when my father charged in the door.

DLM: Now what kind of a pistol?

JC: It's a .22 pistol.

DLM: And how many rounds does it hold?

JC: I think it will hold 10. It's a semi-automatic pistol. It's like a target pistol.

DLM: So it's a clip, magazine?

JC: Yeah, it's got a magazine in it.

DLM: Okay.

JC: I believe he was just loading bullets in the magazine when my father walked in.

DLM: Okay. And he said the .22?

JC: Yeah, he said he used the .22. It's the only gun he's got that will take three bullets.

DLM: Okay. And did he say what—was he planning on using it while he was loading it, or…?

JC: I think he was just angry, and he was basically, you know, "Go away." I think it was intended to be a threat. And my father probably didn't believe him and decided to call him on it.

DLM: Did he say that?

JC: He didn't. No, this is an assumption.

DLM: Okay.

JC: My brother said my dad just started yelling at him, and then my brother pulled the trigger.

DLM: Were they in the shop?

JC: I don't know. He wasn't clear. I'm guessing that my brother was in the shop. Because if he was saying he was loading it, he would have been near his gun safe, which is in the far corner from the door.

DLM: Yeah, okay. So how many times did he say he fired the pistol?

JC: He said he pulled the trigger. That was all he said. He never clarified how many times he pulled the trigger.

DLM: Did he say he pulled the trigger at your father, or he just said, "I pulled the trigger"?

JC: He said, "I pulled the trigger."

DLM: Okay.

JC: Yeah, he didn't clarify. And until I got up and wandered over there I hoped he meant it was like a warning shot, but…

DLM: In your conversation at home, while you were at the picnic table, did he indicate your father was dead?

JC: Yeah.

DLM: How did he word that when he said it?

JC: I asked him, "What did you do?" And he said, "I shot him and he is dead."

DLM: Those were his words?

JC: Those were his words, yeah. My brother, I don't know if it's documented or not, but about six years ago he got into a car accident, and he had some brain damage. So his vocabulary is not the same, not like what everyone else's is.

DLM: Okay.

JC: And a few minor impulse control issues and stuff like that.

DLM: Oh.

JC: But I'm not entirely sure how he meant it.

DLM: Okay. But from the conversation you were having, what was your assumption that he meant?

JC: That he had pulled the trigger and shot him.

DLM: Your father?

JC: Yeah.

DLM: Was he inside or outside of the building?

JC: He was mostly outside of the building. His feet were in the doorway...

DLM: So was his upper body outside?

JC: His upper body was outside, but probably from halfway up his ankles, halfway up his shin, was inside the door, give or take.

DLM: Okay.

JC: And the rest of him was outside.

DLM: Okay. Alright. And did you see any wounds or anything?

JC: I didn't, but he was lying face down, and I didn't want to disturb the body.

DLM: Okay.

JC: I checked for a pulse. There was none. And there was a lot of blood pooled out of his mouth. At which point, I couldn't see any particularly valid reason to mess with anything that the police were gonna want to see.

DLM: Okay. Now, I just want to go a little bit into the history with your father here...

JC: There is a history there, yes.

DLM: Describe that to me?

JC: Where would you like me to start?

DLM: Wherever you would like to.

JC: Growing up, he was physically abusive to my mother. And verbally, mentally, emotionally abusive, to me and my brother. As we got older, he stopped with me, mostly because I got bigger than him and he didn't think he could beat me up. And as he got older, he became basically—we didn't worry about it as much. I was a firm proponent of, "Don't live there." But my brother and my mother are both extremely attached to the farm. It's an emotional, not a rational, attachment to the place. And so they were willing to more or less deal with him rather than move. And as he got older, it was less abusive and more just irrational. He would pick fights for no reason. And he would, you know, he'd bad mouth people for no apparent reason. With me, he was always very chummy, I guess would be the word. You know, like when someone wants a favour how they act?

DLM: Right.

JC: That is how he acted towards me. But my brother always got the verbal berating, treated poorly. And it was not uncommon for it to happen. Like being chased around with a tractor or something like that. Or being threatened to be beat up. It's not the first time it's happened...

DLM: Where he'd chase your brother specifically?

JC: Yeah, he would just go irrational. With me he wouldn't do it, because I wouldn't run. The thing was my brother isn't as strong as I am physically.

DLM: Yeah.

JC: And he's half paralyzed. He's got hemiparesis on his right side. His entire right side is half paralyzed. Like, he can't bend his fingers properly and stuff, from when he was injured.

DLM: Right.

JC: So my dad isn't scared of him, wasn't scared of him. He had no fear of pushing my brother around. Pushing my brother literally to, you know, the limits of what he could stand.

DLM: Right.

JC: And then being happy when my brother got angry. It was basically his method of proving that he was superior and more powerful. In control. It was a control issue thing. I saw it, but I wasn't around it, because I lived far enough away.

DLM: Right.

JC: And I've talked to them about it. And the whole premise was, as bad as it kind of sounds, we weren't.... I don't normally do this much talking. The idea of my father dying isn't a terribly sad idea. I'm not terribly broken up that my father is dead. I'm very, very upset that my brother did it.

DLM: Okay.

JC: Would be the honest, straight-up fact... Like, it's been one of those situations of, no one likes him but we tolerate him.

DLM: Right.

JC: Because there was no way he was ever gonna leave. And they didn't want to leave. And so they basically, they came to a sort of detente. Where they just, everyone just kind of left it alone...

DLM: You indicated when you described it that, when your brother told you that your father went after him with a tractor, he chased him with the tractor, that's not overly surprising to you?

JC: No. It's not the first time it's happened.

DLM: Did your brother tell you of similar incidents that happened?

JC: I've seen similar incidents in the past.

DLM: With your brother alone?

JC: Yeah.

DLM: Anyone else?

JC: He used to do it to my mother before she got hurt, but since she's been in a wheelchair he couldn't get away with that.

DLM: Right.

JC: Mostly because, you know, he's not going to prove anything there. He did it with me till I was about 15. And then we had a bit of a throw down, and after that he stopped trying it on me, except occasionally to push my buttons.

DLM: Okay.

JC: My method of dealing with it was to tell him to go to hell and just leave.

DLM: Right.

JC: And then like a day later he would be fine again. And he'd have no idea why you were mad.

DLM: Okay.

JC: Yeah… There is a long history there, but it's never, ever come close to going this far.

DLM: Has your brother ever mentioned that, or talked about it with you?

JC: Not in a serious manner. It's like, you know, kind of like, I should shoot him, but he's laughing when he says it, not serious when he says it.

DLM: Right.

JC: And the response is, we'd all like to, but that is not the proper way to handle it.

DLM: Yeah.

JC: And it never crossed my mind that it would happen… My response to it is, walk away, ignore it. But I have different methods of dealing with him than he does. Like, my father knew that if he pushed me too far I'd sell my house and move.

DLM: Okay.

JC: You know, I didn't care. But my brother loves the farm and wants to spend, you know, wanted to spend the rest of his life there. And my father knew that, so he had a lever to use against my brother… When he wanted to push his buttons… Any time my brother did something my father disapproved of, in any way, shape or form, he'd say, he was gonna go burn the farm down or destroy it or something like that… It was one of those weird,

weird things. I, me personally, could do no wrong, but my brother could do no right…

After my brother's accident he was in a coma for weeks… He sustained major brain damage in certain areas… My mother would have a better understanding of the medical history… but he shattered his leg. His right leg is about this much shorter than his left: 3/4 of an inch… His right arm doesn't work quite right. He has trouble remembering the words for things.

DLM: So there was some mental damage?

JC: Yeah, there was some mental damage. His reaction time is about a third a normal person's.

DLM: Okay.

JC: So you have to be careful working around him, because where a normal person will see something coming and get out of the way, he won't, and various other things like that.

DLM: Okay. Did you notice a difference in his mental capacity since the accident, aside from his slow reaction times?…

JC: Since the accident? Yes, he has changed dramatically.

DLM: How so?

JC: He used to be a farrier, a horse shoer, and he travelled around with the chuckwagons. He loved to travel and do his thing. After his accident, he couldn't do it anymore. And he couldn't do, he liked to do ironwork art and stuff like that before… he couldn't do any of this, because his dominant right hand didn't work. You can tell it bothers him, but he's never been the type to really let it get him down. Like, he just has the attitude that life goes on, and he's going to continue doing what he needs to. You know, if he can't do one thing, he's gonna do something else, and so he's gotten into doing other things that he can do, you know, carpentry, little bits here and there…

DLM: Okay. Is there anything in his temperament or demeanor that would be different from, say, a normal person that didn't sustain the injuries he did?

JC: He doesn't think things through as well as most people do. Like, a lot of the time when he'd be wanting to do something,

I'd have to stop him and go, have you thought this through, you know… So his impulse control, I guess, isn't what it used to be.

DLM: Okay. Can you briefly describe how he was after, after this incident today?

JC: Um, it just, he was… My brother would get very angry with my father, and understandably so, but he would always be visibly upset. Whereas today when I got there he was calm and almost peaceful.

DLM: Right.

JC: And that's unusual, at least that's unusual for him, in his normal demeanor.

DLM: Alright.

JC: But I mean, I guess I've never seen him in this situation before, either… And he was just calm and relaxed. I'm far more agitated than he was.

DLM: How do you feel about all this? How it all unfolded? What are your thoughts? You know them both far more than I do.

JC: As bad as it sounds, I'm not that upset that he's dead. But I'm incredibly upset that my brother did it.

CHAPTER 16

RIDING IN JUDY'S truck, we passed Jay's truck parked about a kilo-metre from home. That was where the RCMP had stopped Mat and Jason and transferred them to separate police cars.

When we got to the cattle guard farthest from our farm, we found it blocked by a police car. Jason asked the officer who was guarding the gate if we could go in to get medical supplies for me, and he explained there were dogs that needed to be looked after as well. While the officer checked with his higher-up, I finally opened my snack bag and offered snacks to everyone in the truck. Carting that bag around was the only thing I'd done all day that felt normal and right. It seemed like a lifetime since I'd left the Mattson farm, but it had only been six hours since I got the phone call from Mat.

A police corporal eventually showed up, to take us down to the farm. I learned later he was the officer who had first talked to Matti and had arranged for Jason to bring Mat out from the farm to meet the police.

I got my supplies from the house while Jason went to look after the rams. Jenny got Tank and Bella from the house she and Mat shared. I fed Wilbur, the house cat, and Laurie's hedge-hogs, which were in a cage in her bedroom downstairs. When I got back outside, Hobo, the hundred-and-ten-pound Great Pyrenees who normally guarded our sheep, tried to crawl onto my lap. He was agitated by all the unusual activity. My van was still parked at the farm, and the corporal gave me permission to take it.

At the time of Sandy's death, Jason had a lovely modular home on one of our quarter sections about six kilometres from the home place. The house was perched high on a hill, with a view of the faraway Rocky Mountains. His place was wheelchair accessible, so I knew I'd be able to get in there to wash, eat, and meet with people. We decided my best option for sleeping would be to stay in my van overnight, since there was a fold-down bed in the back. I could run an extension cord to the house for my electric blanket. I backed up as close as I could get to the little cement pad a group of us had helped Jason pour at the base of his wheelchair ramp the summer before. My van door opened onto gravel, but it was level. Once I unloaded on my lift, I didn't have far to go before I was on concrete and could roll up the ramp to Jason's door.

We'd no sooner got to Jason's house than people started arriving. It felt as if we were in a disaster zone, with every-one stepping in to answer phones, make coffee, and hug me or Jenny. I took Jason's cordless phone and went down to his bedroom, closed the door behind me, pulled my address book out, and started phoning Sandy's brothers and sister. I had no idea what their reactions would be, but as I worked my way down the list of seven siblings, I was relieved. Even though they were all as shocked as the rest of us, each of them reacted with concern for Mat.

While I was making those calls, Jay took a call from the RCMP on his cellphone. They informed him that the charges against Mat had been changed from second-degree to first-degree murder. At the time I had no idea what that meant, and neither did Jason.

Jenny went home with her parents that evening. I under-stood her need to be with them. They were just average, unsus-pecting people—Judy had been an employee at Home Depot for a decade, and Denis was a heavy-duty oilfield mechanic. They'd been yanked out of their normal day with the news that their son-in-law of less than a month was in jail for shooting and kill-ing his father.

After everyone had left for the night, Jason helped me get out to my van. It had been raining, and his parking area was soft and difficult to roll my wheelchair on. He was worried about leaving me out there, but I assured him I'd be fine. I had my cell-phone with me and I'd call him if I had a problem.

I got on my wheelchair lift and raised it to a level where he didn't have to stoop to hug me. Jason held me while I cried,

"We'll get through this, Mom," he comforted me. "We've had tough times before. Try to get some sleep now. I'll see you in the morning."

When I got into the van, I transferred over from my wheelchair to my commode chair, then transferred to the fold-down bed. I put on my warm long-johns and tee-shirt, then snuggled down in my cozy blankets. The air was cold and clammy, and I was thankful to have a warm, dry spot to sleep. But I'd only lain there for a few minutes before the thoughts started bombarding me. Memories of incident after incident of Sandy's peculiar and abusive behaviour.

Using the grabber I'd left within arm's reach, I pulled my wheelchair toward me. I took my pen and notebook out of the pouch on the back of the chair and started making notes in the dim glow of the van's interior light.

I wrote about how Sandy had been getting increasingly volatile.

I wrote about him buying a crippled horse with damaged lungs because he was infatuated with the young lady who was selling it. He vowed he'd shoot it, and he was wildly infuriated when he found out I'd instructed Matti to take the horse back where it came from. Shooting an animal he'd just paid $2,500 for, and dumping its body in the bush, was preferable to the humiliation he'd feel if he had to acknowledge making a mistake.

I wrote about the way Sandy had treated my visiting fifteen-year-old great-nephew, threatening to beat Derrek up and run him off if I didn't toe the line.

I wrote about Sandy's numerous threats to break my neck, saying he'd hang but it would be worth it to see me die first.

I wrote about him smashing a young cow to death with his quad a few summers before, because he was angry with her for not going where he wanted. He left her calf to die beside her, then hauled them both off to the bush with the tractor.

I wrote about the way he had targeted and tormented my young dog, Glen, chasing and choking it until it cowered and peed itself.

I wrote about his extreme reaction to the phone calls from his mysterious favourite niece, who'd called the house a number of times trying to get hold of him over the past month.

I wrote of how Mat and Jason and I had all grown so used to watching our backs, how we took Sandy's craziness in stride and just tried to keep our distance from it.

❧

On Saturday morning, Jenny came back out to Jay's, saying she needed to be with us. She was very emotional, sobbing one minute, then pulling herself together and insisting, "We can't let him do this. We can't let him destroy us!" I knew what she meant: Sandy still had the potential to destroy her and Matti, even though he was dead.

Jason's friend Christina from Edmonton had been on the road when Jay phoned to let her know Matti was in trouble. He told her she might want to forget about coming over, but Christina said, "I'm halfway there. I'll keep coming. Maybe I can help out." She had no sooner arrived at Jay's empty house that Friday afternoon than the RCMP called her cell and summoned her to Grande Prairie for questioning. Of course, she knew nothing. She hadn't even met any of us yet. Rather than hightail it back to Edmonton when the cops were finished with her, she went to Jay's house and made supper.

Even at that early stage of the journey, I was awed by the support everyone was offering. Saturday at Jason's was spent with people coming and going. There were dozens of phone calls from concerned friends and family. Jason was the main liaison with the RCMP. I either sat at the table on my wheelchair or lay on the couch in Jay's living room. I broke down several times and cried openly, which was unusual for me.

Roy Carter had spoken with Mat at the jail, and he had confirmed that Mat had not intended to hit Sandy. His focus had been on getting the gun to fire as a way of making his father stay away from him. The fact that Mat was a terrible shot with any firearm was common knowledge. It was actually a running joke at our place: whatever Mat was aiming at was the safest thing around. We knew even if he'd actually been aiming for Sandy, he would never have hit him. Nonetheless, I was thankful to hear Roy's assurance that Mat hadn't been the aggressor.

The weather had turned bad the night before, and it continued to drizzle rain all day Saturday. People gathered around

Jay's big dining room table, brainstorming about what we could do to help Mat. In our ignorance, we thought we might be able to visit him at the jail, maybe even take him some of the fresh carrots Ruth Finch had brought. It was a surreal time, and I was thankful to have the support of such strong friends. It was the third time these people had stepped in to pick up the pieces when my life was hit by disaster.

On Sunday morning, the police gave us permission to go to the farm to check on things and feed the animals. They agreed that since I was unable to use a tub or shower that wasn't adapted for me, I could have a bath in my own house. Jason, Jenny, and I headed over together.

As we were driving into the yard, we could see the signs of things happening exactly the way Matti had described them to Jason. It made the hair stand up on the back of my neck. I could almost visualize the intensity of what had taken place. We could see where Mat had been working with the bobcat and where he had suddenly taken a fast, sharp turn to get behind the harrows, then bailed out and run. The bobcat door had been left wide open. There were skid marks on the driveway from his tires turning sharply, and the bobcat was jammed between the big set of harrows and a barbed-wire fence.

As we drove by the scene, I recalled the time Sandy had chased me with a tractor on the other side of that fence. It was a crisp, cold day, the first winter we had cattle. I was on the ground with a pitchfork, peeling off the moldy outsides of the big round bales. Sandy was delivering them to me one by one with the front-end loader on the tractor. I can't remember what it was, but I did something to piss him off. Maybe I was standing in the wrong spot, or I'd taken the strings off a bale the wrong way. It could have been anything. In response, he had lunged at me with the tractor as I struggled to move in the deep snow. I took off running on a trail heading east, knowing that if I stepped off the trail I'd bog down.

Whipping the tractor around, Sandy had come after me down the trail. My heavy winter clothes and boots weighed me down, and I realized I'd made a mistake thinking I could outrun him. The snow was like sugar under my feet. I couldn't get traction on it. I could feel and hear him closing in on me. I bailed off it into some brush as he thundered over the spot where I'd been running a split second before. Sandy didn't look back as he roared off toward the shop, revving the tractor madly.

As I thought of him cornering Matti behind the harrows, I recalled the terror I had felt that day. My bones had felt like water, and my body was sapped of the ability to move. I'd lain in the brush panting, fighting the urge to throw up.

Sandy never spoke of the incident, and I didn't want to trigger another rampage by reminding him of it. But even after I broke my back, I remained fearful when I heard Sandy coming with a tractor. On my power wheelchair, I'd race for a safe spot where I could get well off the road or behind something. I didn't ever trust him not to run me down.

Farther down the driveway that Sunday, we could see the four-wheel-drive tractor parked with its door wide open, where Sandy had stopped and jumped out to continue on foot to Matti's shop. No one ever left a tractor door open at our place. Sandy was fanatical about that. I could sense his rage by looking at the skid marks on the road and seeing that tractor door swinging in the breeze.

Hobo was nervous as he came toward us. He went into a giddy frenzy when he realized who we were. We could see that someone had been tending him, because he had fresh food and water, but clearly he knew something was terribly wrong.

While I was having a bath, Jay and Jenny made their rounds and did what chores needed to be done. They didn't go near Matti's shop, where the shooting had taken place. That was still regarded as part of the crime scene by police. That afternoon Laurie showed up at Jay's place with the motorhome. She set up kennels for the four border collies she had with her, and two more kennels for Tank and Bella, who'd been tied under Jay's porch. Then she joined us in the house.

⌘

Roy Carter told us that at the police station on the day of the shooting, he had been disturbed and affronted by the situation. After he spoke with Matti, it was clear to Roy that the homicide cops were trying to mould Mat's testimony to fit their version of what had taken place. As we would learn later from the transcripts and videotapes of the interrogation, the police continually told Matti they were on his side and the lawyers weren't. The lawyers were just in it for the money, they said. They tried over and over to put words into Mat's mouth as they interrogated him on Friday afternoon and evening.

Roy was a civil lawyer with no experience in criminal law, but there was no one else on the spot to help Mat. Everyone was gone for the long weekend, and Dave Cunningham, though he'd agreed to take the case, was in Edmonton. With the full support of his wife, Allana, Roy stepped in and began the long, arduous journey of ensuring that the true story emerged.

Roy looks deceptively casual in his relaxed shirts and blue jeans. He's average sized. His dun-coloured hair grows down to his collar, and a mustache-goatee combo adorns his face. All of us were about to learn that beneath that casual look lay a brilliant mind and a fierce determination. I'd never known Roy's father, Adley, who died young, but his mother, Aimee, in her eighties by then, had always been an inspiration and a friend to me. People like Aimee Carter were one reason I had so stubbornly refused to move away from the area. I was determined not to forfeit my friends and my community.

Allana Carter, Roy's wife, was the epitome of class. A tiny woman with a huge presence, she ran a business in the city but was a farm girl at heart. Roy and Allana's twelve-year-old daughter, Alle, kept them busy escorting her to show-jumping practice and competitions. Alle took after both her parents in her style, grace, athletic ability, wit, and good looks. All three of them were about to devote a year of their lives to saving Mat.

From the beginning, Roy stressed strongly to Mat that he should not talk to anyone but his lawyer. The police were not there to be his friends. But everyone who knew Mat was aware of his trusting nature. He'd always been that way, but since his brain injury, he'd been trusting and open to a fault. Most people in Mat's situation would be tuned in to self-preservation, but he didn't grasp that what he said could be used against him. In his mind, it was obvious what had happened, and he couldn't imagine anyone questioning it.

On the morning after the shooting, Mat was interrogated by a constable from the Edmonton Major Crimes Unit for about two hours. The constable convinced him to go to the farm to do a video re-enactment of what had happened. He told Mat he would be able to see Jenny that way, and said that the video would help police to sort things out.

Mat believed the police were trying to help him. He was feeling better now that the police had given him some clothes to wear, rather than leaving him to shiver in the thin cotton gown with no socks or underwear he had worn all afternoon and evening on Friday, then slept in.

The constable brought up the name of James Roszko, the hardcore criminal who had killed four Mounties in 2005, saying he knew Mat was not a killer like Roszko. He said to Mat, "I know you're a good guy, and you want to do the right thing, and the right thing is to be honest."

Underneath it all, the constable was contriving to get enough evidence to charge Mat with first-degree murder: planned, intentional, cold-blooded killing.

Roy Carter had no plans to go to the detachment on Saturday. He felt he'd done everything he could for the time being. He'd warned Mat expressly the night before not to talk to the police until he spoke first with Dave Cunningham, the lawyer who would be representing him. But Allana Carter was uneasy about Mat being left alone at the jail. She felt something wasn't quite right, and she insisted Roy go in to see Mat again. They drove from their farm to the jail together.

The Carters arrived just after lunchtime. After arguing with the cops for fifteen minutes, Roy finally convinced them to let him see Matti. He soon discovered that they were preparing to go to the farm to do a reconstruction. He knew that would be a disaster. He'd seen the cop cars lined up outside like it was Grand Central Station.

Mat told Roy the police had promised he could see Jenny if he went to the farm. Roy knew there was no way Jenny would be there, considering it was still a crime scene. Roy became desperate to impress upon Mat that he must not go to the farm. If he did, Roy told him, he could be looking at twenty-five years in prison. As Roy told us later, he understood that Mat was simply too meek to survive such an environment. Roy had seen his college friend destroyed by a maximum-security prison. He knew what he was talking about. "In desperation," Roy explained to me later, "I asked Mat to listen to me closely as to what would happen if he went on the planned trip after I left. Mat looked at me with his eyes wide, as he does, and I said, 'If you go, it will be the last time you cross the Wapiti River for twenty-five years. The next time you cross the Wapiti, it will have twinned bridges, there will be street lights at Grovedale, your mom will be dead, Jenny will be remarried, and your child in the womb will have graduated from college and not know you. When you get to the farm, it will be owned by strangers.'"

"For the first time, I could see fear in his face," Roy recounted to me. "He asked me if I thought that was all true. I said it was, and repeated that I was his only friend in the building."

When Roy asked Mat what he was going to do once Roy left, Mat said, "Nothing. I'll just say I'm not going on the trip."

"That's not good enough," Roy told him. "You need something to do."

Mat answered, "Okay. I'll do exercises in my cell this afternoon."

As Roy was leaving the detachment, he saw the constable from the Edmonton Major Crimes Unit standing with several other detectives and a video crew that had been brought in from Edmonton. The police were clearly upset about the delay.

The constable asked Roy, "Is the kid still going to talk?"

Roy replied, "I don't know. You go ask him."

Roy had no idea if Mat would be strong enough and resist the pressure to go to the farm with the police. It was only later, through the disclosure, that he would learn Mat kept busy doing exercises in his cell for nearly two hours while the police tried to convince him to go on the trip to the farm. Mat stood his ground and refused.

CHAPTER 17

Matthew Gordon CRICHTON
1st Degree Murder
2010-1080663
CASE SUMMARY

Grande Prairie R.C.M.P. General Investigation Section. With information as of September 3, 2010
Accused: Matthew Gordon CRICHTON (DOB 1983-01-14)
1st Degree Murder (S. 235(1) of the Criminal Code)
Summary:

On September 3rd, 2010 at approximately 11:56 hours Matthew CRICHTON (the accused) called 911 and spoke to a Northern Alberta Operational Communication Centre (NAOCC) operator stating that he had just shot his 73 year old father. The accused further stated that he had put up with his father for 27 years and has had enough. The accused stated that he has since locked the gun away in the safe.

Grande Prairie Rural, Municipal, Police Dog Service and GIS members attended to a staging area a few miles from the scene, which is located approximately 19 km west of Grovedale, Alberta.

The accused was contacted on his cell phone by Police. He was calm, co-operative and stated that he would not be any trouble toward Police. Police later learned that the accused's brother Jason had attended the scene as he had found out what had transpired. Police were able to arrange for Jason Crichton to drive the accused out to meet Police safely away from the scene.

The accused was arrested and taken into custody without incident. The accused and Jason were transported back to the Detachment. The property was cleared for public and police safety.

Victim Alex Crichton was located [lying] in the prone position outside a garage door. He was assessed and it was determined that he was deceased. The property was then secured for a search warrant and subsequent examination by the Grande Prairie Forensic Identification Section.

The accused and his father (victim) have had a very unstable relationship since the accused was a child. The accused alleges that his father has a bad temper and has been physically and verbally abusive towards him and his mother.

The accused lives on the same property as his mother and father near Grovedale, Alberta, with his new wife. The accused was recently married to Jennifer Crichton, on August 22nd, 2010. On September 2nd the accused and his wife returned from B.C. after their honeymoon. Jennifer Crichton is approximately three months pregnant with their child.

On Friday, September 3rd, 2010 the accused was on the family property fixing the septic system with a bobcat (construction equipment) by dumping loads of gravel as there had been drainage problems. The victim approached the accused and started yelling at him and flipped out as he disagreed with what the accused was doing. The accused tried to push the victim out of the way with the bobcat and the victim said, "You son of a bitch."

The victim went and got a nearby tractor, and as the accused was coming back with a load of gravel, he saw the victim coming quickly down the road towards him. The accused was fearful and drove the bobcat behind a nearby harrow (farm equipment) to safely enable him to get off of the bobcat and get ready to run. The victim approached him on the tractor and the harrows kept the victim away from the accused.

The victim stated, "I just wanna talk to you, and get your ass over here." The accused then ran and the victim chased, however was slower.

The accused ran into the shop and obtained the combination for the safe, which he wrote on his hand. The accused then proceeded to open the safe and obtained a .22 cal pistol, the accused loaded three shells into the clip.

The victim came running into the shop. There was some banging and crashing. The victim came in and said something to the effect of, "What are you doing? Get over there and fix that."

The accused stated, "I'm getting a gun." The victim said something to the effect of "Bullshit!"

The accused pointed the gun. It took some time to get the safety off. He fired two times and nothing happened. The gun fired the third time as the victim turned away from the accused. The victim fell to the ground. The accused was inside the shop and the victim was near the door when he fired. The accused did not see where the victim was hit. The accused walked past the victim who was just [lying] there. The victim was not moving or saying anything. .

At approximately 11:56 hours, the accused called 911 and stated that he had just shot his 73 year old father. The accused stated that he had been putting up with his shit for 27 years. The accused provided his full particulars and address to the operator, as well as driving directions to the location.

The accused stated that there was nobody else on the property and that his father was deceased. The accused stated that he was going to lock the firearm up in the safe and would not cause any problems to Police.

The accused called his mother Holly CRICHTON and stated that he was sorry to ruin her holiday but he had just shot her husband. She was shocked and thought he was joking. The accused said he had called 911. Holly stated that she would be there as soon as possible.

At approximately 12:15 hours the accused's brother Jason CRICHTON received a call from his mother Holly. Holly told Jason that the accused had shot his father and she didn't think that he was joking. Jason immediately left his work place heading to the family property. Jason called the accused and told him that he was attending. The accused stated that he had shot his father, he locked the gun up and that Police were attending. As Jason got closer to the property, he saw several Police cars staging near the property. Jason called the accused and told him that he wanted him out in the open as he was concerned for the accused's safety. As Jason pulled in, he could see the accused sitting at a picnic table eating a granola bar and drinking a juice box.

The accused told Jason what had happened and that his father was dead. He assessed the victim and could not find a pulse. His face was purple and there was blood coming from his mouth.

At approximately 12:39 hours, Cpl M. Bennett spoke to the accused on his cell phone. The accused stated that the victim was deceased, the weapon was locked away and the accused had no further weapons and there were no other people on the property.

Cpl Bennett then spoke to Jason CRICHTON and arrangements were made with Jason to drive the accused safely away from the property to meet with the Police. Jason and the accused were stopped on Township road 694 just west of the Crichton property and taken into Police custody by Cst C. Chornomydz and Cst A. Janzen without incident. At approximately 13:07 hours the accused was searched by Cpl Simpson. Cst B. Boychuk took over and formally arrested the accused for Murder, read his Charter Rights and Police caution. The accused was then transported to the Grande Prairie Detachment by Cst D. Hyde and Cst B. Boychuk.

Members immediately attended the scene with Police Dog Service and cleared all buildings located on the property. The victim was assessed by members and Emergency Medical Services. The victim did not have a pulse, was not breathing and his skin was discolored reddish blue. There was blood on the victim's nose, mouth area and pooling on the ground. There were no obvious signs of trauma or injury upon initial survey. There were no signs of life and the victim was pronounced deceased.

The victim was found fully clothed [lying] in the prone position outside of a door of a shop near the accused's residence. The scene was then secured by Police for the preparation of a search warrant. At 13:55 hours the accused arrived at the Detachment. He was photographed by the Forensic Identification Section, his clothing was seized and Gun Shot residue (GSR) samples were obtained from the accused. Photos of the accused's hands were taken as the combination for the safe had been written on the accused's left palm.

At 14:19 hours Cst B. Boychuk obtained an audio, videotaped cautioned statement from the accused. The accused provided a full confession to shooting his father Alex Crichton with a .22 caliber pistol. The accused provided an outline of the family's troubled history and the details of the events which led to the accused shooting his father.

On Saturday, September 4th, 2010 a Search Warrant was obtained and executed at the Crichton property by Investigators and Members of Forensic Identification Section. The scene was videotaped and photographed. A single spent .22 cal rimfire casing was located on the interior floor of the shop near to where the victim was found [lying] outside an exterior door. Members were able to open a locked safe which was inside the shop by utilizing the combination provided by the accused. A .22 cal semi-automatic pistol was located inside the safe. Several other long guns were located on the property and seized. On Tuesday, September 7th, 2010 an autopsy was conducted on Alex Crichton at the Edmonton Medical Examiner's office. The cause of death was determined to be a single gunshot wound to the neck by a small caliber firearm.

CHAPTER 18

ON MONDAY, SEPTEMBER 6, three days after the shooting, the police told Jenny and me we could move back to the farm. By that time, Roy Carter and Dave Cunningham were already developing a game plan. They realized how dire Mat's situation was, even though we still didn't. Over the weekend Roy had lined up Mike Head, our friend and neighbour, to fly over the farm in his helicopter and take pictures. Roy's brain was in overdrive, trying to anticipate all of the angles. He wanted to document where and how the bobcat and tractor were parked before anything got moved.

On September 8, five days after the shooting, a group of us met with defence attorney Dave Cunningham at Roy and Allana's house: Jenny, Jason, Brian and Sherry Lofstrom, Derek Lofstrom, Roy and Allana and Alle Carter, Jarin and Amber Carter, Wayne and Paulette Patterson, and me.

Allana had a lovely buffet supper set up, and we ate as we talked. I had no appetite, but I knew I couldn't allow myself to fall apart, so I ate what I could.

"You're going to need money," Paulette Patterson said. "Wayne and I will plan a fundraiser for Matti. We'll get you the money you need."

It's complicated to be the recipient of a fundraising effort. Your emotions range from gratitude to embarrassment and everything in between.

After I was paralyzed in 1996, my first reaction had been that I would bounce back and not need help from anyone. I had no idea at the time that my injury would completely change my life. I'd spent my life working with horses, and a large part of our family income was dependent on my riding. I couldn't fathom not being able to pull my own weight. But the only skill set I possessed had instantly become useless to me.

I'd trained and ridden racehorses for Paulette and Wayne Patterson for years before my accident, and worked side by side with them on numerous community fundraising events. We had a close bond of mutual respect. Wayne served as president of the Grande Prairie Racing Association while I was vice-president. Paulette, with her wonderful sarcastic sense of humour, was the announcer at our summer race meets.

As I lay in the hospital, Paulette and other friends convinced me that if any one of them was in the same situation, I would unquestionably help in every way I could. That's the way things are done in the north, and in any community: people help people. Everyone needs money to survive. I set aside my pride and agreed to accept their help. Paulette and Wayne were heavily involved in assisting me once I got home. Paulette was also on the board for housing for people with disabilities in Grande Prairie, and she'd assured me she would find me a place to live if I ever chose to leave the farm.

I had an easier time accepting help for Mat after his accident. My own experience as a paraplegic had taught me how being disabled affects your ability to thrive. I knew that Mat might be completely disabled, and that his quality of life would be even more bleak if he had nothing. I was thankful for the benefit fundraiser Paulette, Wayne, Sherry, and others organized. I knew it would give Mat a leg up, whatever direction his life was headed in.

I had watched Paulette struggle with health issues for years, and I'd been humbled by her goodness and determination. Now, despite her own struggles, she was prepared to once again organize a massive event for Mat.

This situation was a different ball game, though, and I weighed the pros and cons of another fundraiser in my mind.

One pro, of course, would be the money. Roy Carter had made a point of telling me from the start that he would not be charging a nickel for his involvement in helping Matti. But I knew the case was going to be hugely expensive, even with Roy's generosity. Dave Cunningham never pulled any punches in letting me know how high the costs might be. I knew I'd find a way to pay him, even if it meant selling the farm.

Another positive effect might be as a show of support for Mat. But if that didn't go well, I feared it would be more than my morale could handle. Much of my strength was coming from the support we were getting, and I was afraid a benefit for our family might attract something negative. I had no idea at the time what the public feeling truly was regarding Sandy's death.

When Derek Lofstrom voiced some of the same concerns, we decided to put the fundraiser on hold for the time being. We'd focus instead on what we could do to help Mat in other ways. Dave Cunningham suggested it would be beneficial to get letters of support from people in the community to present at Mat's bail hearing. He and Roy had already put together a draft request, and the group agreed it was perfect.

The letters were not intended to elicit opinions about whether what Mat had done was right or wrong. Their main purpose was to prove to the bail judge that Mat did not have a violent nature. There was never any argument about the fact that he had shot his father.

Sandy's body had been sent to Edmonton for an autopsy. On September 9, the RCMP called to tell me that his remains would be returned to Grande Prairie, where a local funeral home would deal with them. I took exception to not being consulted on the matter. Roy assured me that the RCMP had no grounds to make this decision, and he arranged for a funeral director he knew in Edmonton to deal with the cremation of Sandy's remains. I consulted with Sandy's siblings, and they all agreed that was the way to go. We opted to keep the funeral small and private and to bury Sandy's ashes at the cemetery where his parents and his brother Allen were buried.

Letters of support for Mat started to pour in to Roy's office: at least 150 during the first week. He had his entire staff working to read and sort them. Roy got a map of the Municipal District of Greenview, our area, and had it enlarged. On the map I marked each location a letter had come from. The locations on the south side of the Wapiti River rapidly filled with colour. Roy forwarded some of the most exceptional letters to me, and it bolstered my spirit to read the heartfelt words people were writing about my son. In the weeks that followed, we would receive more than 260 letters of support for Mat from friends and neighbours attesting to his character and expressing the view that he should be released on bail pending trial.

Mat was being held in the Peace River Correctional Centre. Eight days after Mat's arrest, Jason, Jenny, and I headed up to see him. Although he'd been able to call us, he was very restricted in what he could say on the phone, and it was hard to tell what kind of shape he was in. On the way to see Mat, however, we were held up by an accident. Mat was able to call Jenny's cellphone from the jail, but the service was sketchy, and every time he connected with her, the phone would cut out. I was distressed, plagued by visions of Mat feeling we'd deserted him. We'd promised to be there and couldn't explain why we weren't.

By the time we finally got to the penitentiary, we were told we'd arrived too late to see Mat. We had no choice but to drive the three hours back home.

The next day, Derek Lofstrom drove to Peace River with Jenny and me. None of us had ever visited a prison before, and we found it disturbing to be there. Once we'd passed through security, leaving our coats and bags in a locker, we were buzzed into the visiting area. We watched through the glass as Mat was ushered by a corrections officer into the prisoner's side.

With his oversized blue prison coveralls tucked into his socks to prevent the legs from dragging on the floor, and black, plastic flip-flops on his feet, Mat looked painfully vulnerable as he limped into the enclosure. There were about a dozen phones attached to the safety glass, spaced about four feet apart. When he spotted us, he headed over to an unoccupied phone station and sat down.

I couldn't get my wheelchair in close enough to reach the phone, so Derek lifted me out of my chair and set me on a stool that was bolted to the floor. He held me there so I wouldn't tip off while I talked to Mat. I was determined to make sure he knew we were all working to get him home, and that we weren't angry with him. Roy and Dave had warned us that everything Mat said would be monitored, so I held a note up to the window for him to read: "You aren't allowed to talk about Sandy to anyone, not even me. You can't say a word. The only people you're to trust are Roy and Dave. They are your only friends."

Mat nodded his head to indicate he understood.

Even with Derek holding me, sitting on the wooden stool caused me extreme pain. I knew I couldn't stay there for long or I would develop a pressure sore. I needed to look after myself through all of this. If I ended up in the hospital, I would be no use to Matti.

After Derek set me back on my wheelchair, he and Jenny each took a turn talking to Mat. When visiting time was up, I asked Derek to set me back on the stool again so I could say goodbye. I said to Mat carefully, aware that other ears were likely tuned in, "I don't know the details of anything, but I know you. We all love you very much. Always remember we're doing everything possible to get you out of here and back home, where you belong." I saw the weight lift off his shoulders, and I knew he was okay. He could see we were there for him.

Jenny's parents drove up with us the next weekend to visit Mat. He was noticeably more frail than he had been the week before, but I was struck by the calm that cloaked him. He had a serene expression on his face as he made his way through the testosterone-charged cluster of prisoners to a vacant phone.

After a few minutes, a fight broke out in the enclosure. Tempers flared, and even visitors were yelling and screaming. People on both sides were smashing phones against the Plexiglas. Guards came into the glassed-in room and escorted out two prisoners who were out of control. Even as this chaos raged around him, Mat sat calmly on his stool and talked to Jenny through the phone.

Much later, once Mat was back home, I asked him if he'd been afraid while he was in prison. He told me that, other than a few times when he was in immediate danger, he hadn't been frightened. "I was surrounded by a bunch of guys who were just like Dad was," he said. "I knew how to deal with them. I just made myself invisible."

CHAPTER 19

WE BURIED SANDY'S ashes on a crisp and sunny afternoon. The striking beauty of the world that day made the event that brought us all together seem even more surreal.

We'd planned to meet Sandy's siblings at the cemetery, about an hour's drive from home. The closer we got to our destination, the more anxious and apprehensive I became. I wondered how it would go. Would people be emotional? Sad? Angry?

We parked at the tiny cemetery, a stone's throw from the highway. I unloaded from my van, and Jason pushed my chair over the grass to where everyone had gathered, near the graves of Sandy's mother and father. As we neared, I saw a cardboard box about fourteen inches square sitting near a small hole that had been dug between the graves. So this is how it ends, I thought. What a sad ending to a life.

Sandy's brother Chris had brought his ashes from Edmonton. One of his sisters-in-law opened a bible. After reading a few verses, she spoke about Sandy for a few moments. She talked about how he had loved horse racing and how he had been a very hard worker, successful at everything he attempted. "But," she added, "we all knew he had a dark side."

When she was done speaking, she asked if anyone else had something they'd like to say. No one stepped forward, and there was an awkward silence. I hadn't planned on speaking, but it didn't seem right to leave without saying a word.

"I guess I should say something," I began hesitantly. Everyone turned toward me. I spoke slowly, forcing my mind to focus. I was incredibly angry. Sandy had caused his own death through his terrible rages. I was tormented by questions I hadn't pondered for years. Why was he so full of fury? Why had he targeted the people closest to him? At the same time, I was stricken with grief. I was mourning for Sandy, and for Mat. Icy claws gripped my brain and squeezed the air from my lungs. I thought of how Sandy's death had the potential to destroy us all. To drag us down into that hole in the ground with him.

Fighting to speak past the bile rising in my throat, I looked at the little cardboard box. "I'm truly sorry Sandy's life had to end like this. He was so talented and capable. He had everything a person could hope for. I've tried to figure out for twenty-nine years what caused him to be so mean to his family, and so angry all the time. I guess that's something I'll never know."

People stood silently digesting my words, then filed slowly away from the graves toward their vehicles. Sandy's brother Jim grabbed my wheelchair push bars to give me a hand getting through the lush mowed grass. As we neared the gravel road winding through the cemetery, he slipped and fell down, pulling my wheelchair on top of him. The mood was lightened for a moment. Everyone had a laugh as we got untangled from the wreck.

After leaving the cemetery, we all went to a Chinese restaurant in Grande Prairie. There too, I was grateful for the show of support from Sandy's family. I couldn't imagine what they were going through, having to process their oldest brother being shot and killed by his son. I'd never been at a Crichton family function without Sandy, and I was aware of how much more relaxed I was without him there.

After we'd finished eating, Jason and one of Sandy's brothers lifted me down the stairs of the café in my wheelchair. As we gathered for our goodbyes on the sidewalk outside, I told the family I'd inform them as soon as I knew when Mat's bail hearing would be. Some of them said they planned to attend. I'd already shown them the brief obituary I'd written to appear in the *Herald-Tribune*, and they'd approved it.

Not long after the obituary appeared, I received an e-mail message from one of Sandy's nieces.

Hello Holly,

My name is Donna (Crichton), Uncle Sandy's niece. I don't know how to say this, so I will just come right out with it. If Matty needs anyone to help with what is happening, I have information that may help.

We have never met, because I have only been up to that area once in the last 30 years, and that was for my mom and dad's 50th anniversary. I talked to Sandy for a few minutes and realized that he hadn't changed in all those years.

I am sorry that you lost a husband and that my dad lost a brother. Maybe in time we can all forgive.

You are in my prayers.

Donna

I had no idea what Donna was talking about, but I definitely wanted to know. I sent her a message saying I'd appreciate anything she could do to help Mat.

The reply I received later that day made my blood run cold.

Aunt Holly,

The information I was talking about was the molesting of his nieces and the beatings he gave Aunt Mary. People know about this, but no one is willing to talk about it. Things have happened in my life because of it, and I think it is time that everyone dealt with how bad things were. If there is anything that I could do to help you or Matty, please let me know.

Please feel free to share this with whomever you think it might help.

Donna

The pieces started tumbling into place in my mind.

For twenty-nine years, I had tried to figure out what caused the man I married to engage in such bizarre episodes of violence. Suddenly I'd discovered at least one of the triggers for his rages.

I had learned to think carefully about every word I said to Sandy, and I was always baffled when he accused me of putting him down. He didn't usually react right away when I made caustic remarks about child molesters. His response always came a few days later in attacks that seemed random at the time. Now I knew some of his violence had been provoked by what I said.

Sandy was all about his image. If he had been exposed as a child molester, the humiliation would have shamed him beyond redemption. I was sure he would sooner have died, or killed someone else, than have his perversions revealed. My stomach churned as I began to digest this new side to the man I'd been married to for nearly thirty years.

I phoned Donna right after receiving her e-mail, and I could hear in her voice that Sandy still had the power to cause her anguish. He had not only sexually molested her, he'd terrified her into keeping it a secret. Even as an adult, she'd been afraid of what he'd do if she revealed what he'd done.

Little did I know at that time, but Donna would be the first of many women to come forward with similar stories.

CHAPTER 20

MAT'S BAIL HEARING was set for October 25. We knew there was a good chance he wouldn't get out. Dave Cunningham had told us it was rare for anyone charged with first-degree murder to be released on bail.

Over and above all the work and worry associated with the pending hearing, we had 170 head of cows with calves at their side scattered across various pastures, and 160 acres of grain crop to take off. I knew we'd have to sell our cows to pay for Mat's lawyer. Plus, with Mat and Sandy gone, there was no way I could look after them. Jim Peel and Jim Lofstrom gathered cows from one pasture, while Laurie Wedler and Bob Finch gathered the remainder, and Bob marketed them for me. I was thankful he'd offered to do the job. Marketing cattle was Bob's business, and I knew he would do the best job he possibly could.

Brian Lofstrom and Ken Ryan combined 80 acres of grain, and we decided the best way to harvest the remainder with the least amount of labour would be to cut and bale it. Then I could sell the bales. Five neighbours—Stan Bulford, Larry Smith, Billy Smith, Danny Williams, and Brian Lofstrom—showed up with hay-bines. They cut the crop, and about ten days later the same crew returned with equipment to bale it. They finished baling on the evening of October 1. I was hugely appreciative. These men were taking time away from their own work and using their own equipment to harvest the crop for us. After the baling was completed, we had a potluck meal out in the field. Many people showed up to join the baling crew for supper. There was plenty to eat, with Crock-Pots and roasters full of food sitting on the tailgates of pickup trucks and on a full-sized fold-up table.

Everyone was keyed up about Matti's situation, and it had been hard-going to get the crop harvested. During supper, the rum and Coke came out. Everyone relaxed, and the stories and laughter started to flow. It was pitch-black by this time, and we were gathered in lawn chairs around a bonfire in the middle of an 80-acre field. Two neighbours saw the fire from the highway and drove out onto the field, thinking our bales were on fire. Once they'd arrived at the bonfire, they stayed and joined the party.

I drew comfort from the companionship, but inside I was intensely frightened and worried. Not a moment went by that I wasn't waiting for the other shoe to drop. I was on constant alert for sirens or for cellphones ringing with more bad news. My entire reality had changed with Sandy's death and Mat's imprisonment, yet everyone else remained the same. It was a fragile space I occupied, and I clung to the solid normality of my friends and neighbours.

We'd sold our lambs in August, but there were still 150 ewes to look after. Laurie took charge of the flock. Jenny was nursing full-time at the hospital. I spent the bulk of my time working feverishly with Dave Cunningham while still attending to the business of the farm. Vern Danielson and Art Verhage filled the woodshed at Mat and Jenny's place. That way, Jenny would have wood for winter if Mat didn't come home. Every day a steady stream of people stopped by to visit or to help us out.

We made sure someone went up to visit Mat every weekend. As a lawyer, Roy Carter was able to see Mat in jail during non-visiting hours. He drove to Peace River several times. He wanted to assure Mat we were all working to get him home, and he was looking for a better understanding of what had happened the day Sandy was shot. Dave Cunningham was the lawyer calling the shots, but Roy worked hard to help Dave piece the story together.

We continued to be amazed at the number of support letters that were arriving. Dave's game plan of proving to a bail judge that Mat was not a threat to society was looking more promising all the time.

To help Dave Cunningham understand the dynamics of Sandy's behaviour, I'd turned my most recent journal over to him. I was taken aback at first when Dave looked at the binder I'd hidden my notes in and chuckled. The title stamped on the front was *Seven Habits of Highly Effective People: Workshop by Stephen R. Covey.* I could see the dark humour. I also gave Dave a cassette that contained a few of Sandy's rants.

By this time, two more of Sandy's nieces, Donna's sisters Shirley and Sharon, had come forward with stories of being repeatedly sexually assaulted by Sandy as children and young women. It was not something they talked about with ease; I could tell it was tearing them up to dredge these horrible memories from the past. I was deeply thankful that they wanted to help Mat, but over the course of many phone calls, I told each of them that, regardless of what happened, they had to do what was right for them. I couldn't stand the thought of pressuring them to put such painful secrets out for all to see if they weren't ready to do so. All three eventually chose to make statements to the lawyers and said they were willing to testify under oath. They felt it was important for them to expose Sandy's true character.

Two letters from local women also arrived along with the support letters for Mat. Both women had been sexually assaulted by Sandy as girls and had carried the effect of that for decades. It hurt me to learn that these women I knew well had been harmed by my husband.

To the Mat Crichton Bail Support Effort:

All of my life I have struggled with feelings of unworthiness. I now see that I made the most important choices of my life under the influence of those feelings and I have paid a terrible price… When Sandy died all the feelings from my experience with him when I was a little girl came to the forefront of my mind for the first time in years. Other than to warn a friend fifteen years ago that he was not to be trusted with her little girls, for more than thirty years I had left my experience with Sandy in the past, tucked neatly away in a hidden corner of my heart… Sandy Crichton was a man who wore many masks. On the outside, to a little girl, he appeared kind and fun-loving and trustworthy. But there was a darker side to him that I got to see up close and personal. Sandy only fondled me the one time, but that was enough… Is Sandy totally responsible for the downward spiral of my adult life? No. He is not. Was he a contributing factor in the way I learned to view myself? Absolutely. Sandy did not have the right to force himself sexually into my life. I was a young, impressionable, trusting child who looked up to and admired him.

For the Mat Crichton Bail Effort:

Is it ever the right time to say that you are glad that someone is dead? That someone, who hadn't even had very much to do with your life for years, is finally gone from your life forever?

I am guilty of this, because I am relieved in a strange way that a certain man is no longer walking on the face of this earth. I only wish that he had "checked out" on his own years ago… I was young when I first met this man. He was mean to people and animals and his temper flared very quickly, cuss words flying from his lips. My dad recently recalled an incident way back when my granddad was still alive.

This man (the now deceased) was beating on a horse to try to get it into a horse trailer and the horse was not eager to enter. Finally, my grandfather had reached his limit (watching this person abuse the horse) and he took the whip that the guy was using. He told the guy that if he struck that horse one more time, he was going to use it on him. My dad then took the halter shank and led the frightened horse into the trailer without incident.

But my real dislike for this man was rooted in my 12-year-old mind, for that was how old I was when he did this to me. I was always afraid of him and I tried to avoid him as much as possible, but we were neighbours, and often he was at our farm, either working with my dad and granddad, or maybe borrowing something…

On this particular day, a bright summer afternoon, I can clearly remember that I was back behind the barn in the little pasture trying to catch the horses... When I was heading back toward the house he grabbed me from behind, and held me with one hand between my legs, and the other one on what wasn't even yet a breast... When he released his hold I went up to the house right away...

Later that evening, I told my mom what had happened. I wanted her to tell me that "he" had been very wrong to have done that to me, and that she would let my dad know, and they would have a word with this person... But, instead, my mom said that I must have been mistaken. That he hadn't meant to grab me where he did, and that I had misunderstood what he had said to me. In reality, she was just not wanting to make waves with "him" and because he was an adult and I was only a kid, it was easier to tell me to forget about it... It didn't really happen.

I thought about how naive and carefree I had been as a child, and it ripped at my heart that someone, worse yet a man I had loved and trusted, had purposely abused vulnerable girls.

All of these women had held these secrets inside themselves for decades, but the hurt they felt at the betrayal of their trust had never diminished. The fact that several of them had told their parents and not been believed made it even worse for them.

With these bombshell revelations about Sandy, my brain started a crazy scramble. Strange, unexplainable incidents from the past suddenly had context and meaning.

Sandy had been receiving odd phone calls for about a month before he died. The first call had come on August 4. Because what transpired was so strange, I'd noted the date on the calendar.

Holly: "Hello?"

Caller, "in a very distinct, sing-song voice, a woman sounding like a little girl": "Is Uncle there?"

"Excuse me?"

"Is Uncle there?"

"I'm sorry, who are you calling for?"

"I'm calling for Uncle!"

"I'm sorry, who is your uncle?"

"Uncle Sandy!"

"Oh, okay. I'm sorry, he's not in right now. Can I take a message?"

"Tell him Sally phoned. His favourite niece. Tell him to call me."

I had no idea who the woman was, but when I told Sandy about her call, he'd muttered under his breath, "What the fuck does she want?"

I didn't think much more about it. It was bizarre, but I certainly didn't want to get caught up in any of Sandy's issues.

I answered calls from the same woman three more times in the month of August. Each time she asked for Uncle and referred to herself as his favourite niece.

After the third call, I asked Sandy, "Who is this lady?"

He snarled, "She's just a flake. Leave it alone."

There was a fourth call, about a week before Sandy died. Since then, there had not been any more.

When I learned about Sandy assaulting girls decades before, I thought again about Sally, the niece who had been calling. I decided to track her down. I was sure Sandy's brother Glen would know who she was.

Once I had Sally's mother's name, I looked up her number. When I reached her, she told me Sally was in a psychiatric institution, and had been in and out of various institutions for most of her life. She gave me the number where Sally could be reached. I wanted to talk to Sally, but I was unsure of how to proceed. I didn't know her, and I would be calling her out of the blue.

The revelations about Sandy's vile history were really messing with my head. I couldn't sleep, and I had trouble eating; my stomach would lurch with every thought I had of him. As horrible as Sandy's violence and physical abuse had been, learning that he was a pedophile was a hundred times worse.

Finally I called the institution where Sally was, and a nurse brought her to the phone. I explained who I was and asked if she'd heard what had happened to Sandy. It stopped me in my tracks when she said, "I was shocked to hear that. I found him to be such a wonderful uncle."

I'd been prepared for Sally to tell me how much Sandy had scared her, like his other nieces had done. I still sensed something disturbing about her connection with Sandy, but I tried to forget about her. I was busy with numerous other leads regarding Sandy's history. I followed up whenever my radar sensed a possible advocate for Mat. I couldn't get Sally out of my mind, though, and I decided that I'd try to talk to her again. I called to ask if I could come and see her. She agreed to meet with me.

A few weeks later, I arrived at the institution as planned. I made my way from my van with a box of TimBits wedged between my knees, and a tray holding two large Timmy's coffees on my lap. As I waited behind locked doors where a nurse stood doing paperwork next to a reception desk, a nicely dressed, middle-aged woman poked her head around an opening next to the nurse, and exclaimed, "Oh! You did come!"

It was obvious she'd been waiting for me. She called out to a different nurse, to come quickly, chattering excitedly that she had company.

The nurse unlocked the door and let me into a large open room where a number of people mingled near a pool table. After spending over a month with Matti in the brain injury ward at the Glenrose Hospital, I understood the protocol of entering a locked facility. I knew I couldn't leave at will; someone would have to let me out again.

The nurse directed us into a small private lounge just off the group area. I set the treats on the coffee table, and Sally settled herself on one of the loveseats.

While she rummaged through the TimBits box, I explained I wanted to talk to her so I could get a better picture of what Sandy was like before I knew him.

Sally began to chat away about how much she loved her Uncle Sandy and how sad she was that he was dead. He'd always treated her special, she said. He took her with him when he went to the grazing lease to check cows, she remembered, and he let her ride his horse Dodger. She was his favourite niece.

"Some other girls said that Uncle Sandy raped them," she

told me, "but they were lying. They were jealous because Uncle liked me best."

Sally had stayed at the farm a lot from the time she was ten years old until she got married, she told me. "Uncle even paid for my wedding!"

I asked her if she knew why her Auntie Mary had left Sandy.

She replied, "Auntie left because Uncle always beat her. I knew he felt glad I always listened to him, and he didn't have to do that to me. Why did she have to make him so mad? My sister would hide under the bed and cry when Uncle tried to get her to go to the farm with him. I couldn't understand why she hated going, but it was okay with me. That way I got Uncle all to myself."

"Why were you phoning Sandy so often just before he died?" I asked her.

"I missed him."

"Did he ever call you back?"

"Yes. He said he'd come and see me, but then he died."

I was sickened by the things I was hearing, and even more sickened by what I imagined the women Sandy had molested thought of me. Did they assume I knew what he was like and I was okay with it? It shook me to the core to realize that behaviour I had always spoken out against so strongly had existed for all those years under my own roof in the person of my husband. There had often been little girls around our place. What if Sandy had molested them? Surely there would have been some sign, something I would have noticed. I had always been ashamed of the way Sandy treated me. Now I felt the shame of what he had done to other people.

A conversation I'd had with an aunt in 1982, the year after Jason was born, came back into my mind with a jolt. My aunt had been criticizing my niece Tracy for her bad behaviour. Saying Tracy had even gone so far as to say that Sandy had molested her when she'd stayed at the farm with us the previous summer. According to my family, my aunt said Tracy had a history of stretching the truth. My aunt thought Tracy was just trying to get attention by telling more lies. I agreed with her at the time that Tracy had been making things up. Sandy would certainly never have messed with a twelve-year-old. Only a creepy pervert would do something like that. Now I thought, *if that's true, if he did molest Tracy, that's why he beat me up a week after she left.* That's when his hatred of me began. For the first time of many to come, in connection with news stories we'd hear, I had verbalized my disgust for pedophiles.

In 1982, I had brushed off Tracy's story about Sandy as coming from a messed-up kid. Now I knew it was very likely he had molested her.

I decided I needed to find her and ask her about the summer she had spent with us. Tracy had dropped off my radar, and it was quite a process to track her down. When I did finally make phone contact with her, I told her what had happened to Sandy and asked if he had tried anything with her the summer she was twelve. The story poured out of her. Tracy recalled in detail how that summer had gone and what Sandy did to her. He had blamed her for what he was doing, and he'd made threats about what would happen if she told anyone. As I listened to Tracy, my stomach churned. While I was happily anticipating our baby and the future we had before us, Sandy was repeatedly molesting Tracy, making her summer at the farm a nightmare.

"I tried to tell a couple of people about it once I got home," she said, "but they called me a liar. They said I should appreciate everything you had done, and to stop making trouble."

"Oh, Tracy," I said, "I'm so sorry. Why didn't you tell me?"

"I knew what he did was wrong," she said. "Anyone would know that. But I didn't want you to hate me or be mad at me. You were my hero. You were the only one who cared about me."

I had thought at the time that a summer at the farm was going to enhance Tracy's life, but it did the complete opposite.

CHAPTER 21

A NUMBER OF other support letters sent on Mat's behalf revealed that Sandy hadn't kept his dark side hidden as well as he thought. Dave Cunningham told us Sandy's molestation of little girls likely wouldn't be admissible in court, because it had nothing directly to do with Sandy getting shot. But, he said, the severe beatings people had witnessed Sandy give his wife, Mary, and his violence toward the girls he had abused, might be.

When I asked Sandy's brother Glen about his memories of Sandy, Glen told me about the three summers he had spent with Sandy as a young teenager after their father died. He agreed to write a statement detailing his experiences. Glen also told me how angry and disappointed he had been when he twice helped me to get away from Sandy, and I ended up back with him both times.

I was shocked by his comments. I had no memory at all of these incidents. Later I realized I must have blocked them from my mind, an unconscious strategy for surviving my years with Sandy. At the time, I simply asked Glen if he could tell me what had happened. He said that both times I had phoned him and told him I had to get away from Sandy, that I was scared he was going to seriously injure or kill me. The first time, Glen said, he had driven me in to the women's shelter in Grande Prairie, then heard a few days later that I was back with Sandy. The second time he had dropped me off at a neighbour's place—he couldn't remember who. Glen was in the loop with the local logging truck drivers at the time, and he told me he'd heard through the grapevine that one of Sandy's good friends had talked me into going home to the farm. After that, Glen said, he decided to stay away. He couldn't stand knowing I kept putting myself back into the same dangerous situation.

Glen said that when I made the choice not to go back to Sandy after my accident, then changed my mind, he saw it as the same old story. When he heard from some cousins that Sandy had told them he was going to an anger management group, Glen recalled that he had just shaken his head. "I knew it was either a flat-out lie," he told me, "or a ploy, and he'd be manipulating them into thinking he was a great guy."

The summer I was in the hospital, Glen told me, there had been a Crichton family reunion. Glen remembered Sandy confronting him there, saying, "You better keep your mouth shut and stay out of my business, or I'll come after you."

Glen had squared off with him and answered, "If you ever come after me, one of us will walk away, and one won't."

Glen knew better than most what kind of person Sandy was, and he was prepared to go to any length to help us prove it to the courts.

The law is fairly black and white on what constitutes self-defence. As Dave Cunningham told us, if Mat had shot Sandy two seconds sooner, before he turned, there wouldn't have been any issue. The kicker was that the bullet was in the back of Sandy's neck. Dave knew he had a monumental task ahead of him defending Mat against the first-degree murder charge, but the first order of business was to get Mat out on bail. He explained that if Matti remained in jail, it could greatly affect the outcome of the trial.

The only hope of saving Mat was to paint a clear picture of the terror and confusion in his shop during those few seconds it took for him to pull that trigger. Dave had to find a way to illustrate the story through Mat's eyes. He asked me to fill him in on anything I could to help him better understand who Sandy was. I felt like a tabloid reporter digging into Sandy's life, but I knew it would paint a far more believable picture if people other than Mat, Jason, and me could attest to what he was capable of.

In Sandy's private papers, I found the divorce records from his first marriage, with the reason for the divorce stated as follows:

The respondent since the celebration of the marriage has treated the petitioner with physical and mental cruelty rendering continued cohabitation intolerable.

The respondent has on numerous occasions subjected the petitioner to physical abuse of varying degrees, verbal abuse of varying degrees, consumed alcoholic beverages excessively on occasion and has an extremely violent temper which made the petitioner very much afraid of him. As a result of the conduct of the respondent the petitioner suffered extreme nervous anxiety and ultimately continued cohabitation was rendered intolerable.

I was haunted by the vision of Mary, a beautiful young girl away from her parents' home for the first time, working as a cook's helper in a remote logging camp. Sandy, a powerful and determined young logger, had no doubt swept her off her feet with his charm. I could also imagine only too well her despair when she got to know the man behind the mask.

Our family doctor also agreed to stand up for Mat at trial. He knew something of the history of Sandy's violence and the implications of Matti's brain injury as well. I knew his word would not be taken lightly. I decided to contact Mat's doctor from the Glenrose Rehabilitation Hospital too. I learned that she had since retired, but she gave me the names of a few other doctors we could contact for support.

The bail hearing was slated for October 25. I had asked Dave if we should try to have a room full of people there, as a show of support for Mat, but he advised me to keep the number to about a dozen. Sometimes judges felt pressured by having a lot of people in the room, he told me. He wanted the judge to be relaxed and thinking only of Matti.

Jason and I, along with Jenny, Jenny's parents, a few close neighbours, and a number of Sandy's family members planned to get to the courthouse an hour before the hearing was scheduled to start. None of us knew the protocol, so we were all very nervous.

The Provincial Building in Grande Prairie is a sprawling complex connected by a covered walkway to the courthouse, which in turn is connected to an RCMP detachment. There was only one wheelchair parking spot at the Provincial Building, but it was free that morning, which I took as a good omen. I clattered along the building's uneven sidewalk for a few hundred metres, then made my way up the concrete ramp to the entry door. The button for the automatic door opener didn't work, but luckily someone behind me reached to pull the door open. There was a lip about three inches high where the concrete had shifted, but the same person helped me get my chair over that.

Once inside, it was easy travelling to the courthouse entry doors.

As I wheeled toward the scanner just inside the door, I realized my Leatherman tool was still in its case, strapped to the side of the footrest on my manual wheelchair. The young sheriff monitoring the scanner offered to hold it for me until after the hearing. He was so pleasant it made me feel a little less anxious.

While the people in our group were getting settled in the waiting area, I decided I'd use the washroom across the hallway. I made my way in through the double doors with no problem, but on the way out I got stuck in between them. That happens sometimes; if the doors are set in a certain way, there isn't enough room to pull the second door open while backing your wheelchair away from it. I was thankful when someone came along to use the washroom and helped me get out.

When we learned that Mat's hearing had been switched from a downstairs room to an upstairs one, we also discovered that the elevator wasn't working. I felt like crying. After my initial good luck at finding a parking spot, I'd been plagued by setbacks because of my wheelchair. But crying or quitting was not an option. There was nothing I could do but wait for the elevator to be fixed. Everyone waited downstairs with me. The elevator was finally repaired and we were still on time for the hearing.

As we waited outside the courtroom, Dave Cunningham came up the stairs wearing a suit and carrying a briefcase. His serious demeanour underscored the dreadful reason we were there. Prior to that, every time I'd seen Dave he was dressed casually in jeans and a shirt. It was easy to picture him out on the ocean sailing his boat. On this day, there was nothing casual about him. He looked like the captain of a warship.

We followed Dave into the courtroom through an imposing wooden door. The only courtrooms I'd ever seen were on television, and the room was smaller than I expected. The carpet was shabby. There were no windows, and the air smelled musty. It was obvious the room had seen a lot of traffic.

When attending a public event, my normal tendency is to sit near the back of the room. I feel uncomfortable being front and centre. But there was no question of that now. I sat at the edge of the front row, directly behind Dave, separated from him by a wooden railing. Dave sat alone at a brown Arborite table, a huge stack of legal books and papers next to his elbow, and an empty chair pulled up beside him.

The prosecutor's table, identical to Dave's, was on the other side of the room. The prosecutor was a young, dark-haired lawyer dressed in an elegant business suit, and she was sorting through her books, while her assistant, a competent-looking young man, sat beside her. *So those are our enemies,* I thought. I glanced at the few people sitting in the spectator seats behind the prosecutor's table, and wondered if they were our enemies as well.

After a few minutes, a sheriff came through a side door with Matti. He held Mat's arm lightly as he guided him into a cubicle set against the wall. Once Mat was seated, the sheriff stood over to one side with his arms crossed.

Mat looked pale and shaken as he glanced toward the gallery where we all sat silently. I hoped he felt comforted to see everyone who had come to support him.

Court was called to order, and the judge, Madam Justice Crighton, was introduced. I was amazed when I heard her name. I prayed she would judge Mat as much by her observation of him as by the words she was about to hear.

As the hearing got underway, the prosecutor seemed intent on proving that Mat had intentionally committed a heinous crime. She insisted he was a dangerous person who should be kept in jail until his trial. She painted Mat in the worst possible colours. He was a cold-blooded murderer, she claimed, and his father a feeble old man.

As I listened to the prosecutor, the immensity of our plight hit me with full force. Terror washed over me in waves. How could this be happening? There wasn't a thing I could do to help my son. It was all on Dave's shoulders now.

I knew Dave wanted to expose as little as possible of his defence strategy at this stage, but as he divulged some of the information he had gathered about Sandy's character, and about Mat's, I could feel a shift in the mood of the courtroom. Dave was painting an entirely different picture of events than the one advanced by the police.

The courtroom was silent as Dave explained how, after Sandy had slapped the cake I was making for Matti's third birthday out of my hands, he had smashed my face into the kitchen counter, grinding it down until my cheek was slashed open and bleeding while the boys cowered beside me. How the two-inch crescent-shaped scar from that day was still visible on my cheek. He told them how, after seeing blood streaming down my face, Sandy had reacted by screaming at me, "You fucking cunt! You cut yourself on purpose to try to make me look bad!" before he stormed out the door. Dave talked about the fact that Sandy had committed violent acts toward his family on an almost daily basis, and that his violence toward Mat had escalated after Mat's accident.

After she had heard all the arguments, Madam Justice Crighton asked that the hearing be adjourned until the next day. She said she wanted time to read all the support letters submitted on Mat's behalf, which Dave had had bound, numbered, and indexed for ease of reference. Mat was escorted out through the side door he had entered, to spend the night in the Grande Prairie jail.

After a stressful, sleepless night, we gathered in the courtroom the next morning to hear what the judge had decided. To our great relief, Madam Justice Crighton granted Matti bail, saying to the crown prosecutor, "I don't know why you keep calling this a heinous crime. It sounds more like a tragedy to me."

That evening Mat, Jenny, and many of the people who had been at the hearing, along with Roy and Allana Carter and Dave Cunningham, came to the farm for a celebratory supper. We were jubilant, for those few hours at least. It had been a gruelling journey so far, and as Dave had reminded me privately, this was just the first small step along the way. There was still a first-degree murder charge hanging over Mat's head.

CHAPTER 22

THE NEXT MORNING, I headed out at eight o'clock as usual to walk my dogs. Our border collies are kennelled unless we're doing something with them, so we're diligent about making sure they get walked and cared for. As I headed down the trail, Mat and Jenny's dogs, Tank and Bella, came charging along. Now that Mat was home again, I knew he wouldn't be far behind.

I stopped my wheelchair. Sure enough, without the hum of my electric motor, I could hear Mat whistling a tune. A second later, he broke into sight around a bend in the trail.

Mat is a habitual whistler, always tweeting out a happy tune around the farm. When I heard him whistling that morning, I thought about one of the first things Dave had said to me when Mat was in Peace River jail: "Tell him not to whistle in there."

When I searched the internet to learn why whistling is taboo in prison, I found a post by "Dodger" on Yahoo. "You do not whistle in prison, #1. Because it is a sign of being happy and you're not supposed to be happy in jail (some of the more hardened inmates find it offensive and trust me you don't want to upset them). #2. "Birds are free, you're *not*." (Kind of the same principle as #1)."

I'd quickly passed Dave's warning along to Mat, and I was relieved when he replied, "I know that, Mom. I saw on a movie once where it didn't end well for a prisoner who whistled in jail."

My heart was full to exploding now. Mat was free, at least for a while, to whistle and walk his dogs again. We carried on down the trail together, with the dogs tearing around, chasing one another through the underbrush. That afternoon I asked Mat to talk me through what happened the day he shot Sandy. It was the first time I'd been able to speak to him alone since he'd been arrested, and I was desperate to hear the story directly from him.

Over the next few days, I helped him to write down what had happened in his own words.

MAT'S STORY

With my brain damage, I always have to think about what I am to do. Sometimes it isn't right anyway. Also, I understand how many people with brain injuries can get irate with society or with life. With me, it is fairly simple. I can't remember names of people or a lot of things. I just laugh at myself and try to do something or talk to somebody to jog my memory. Just operating during the day takes constant thought.

Dad could easily throw a wrench into my constant thought. I learned rather than get mad and yell, I would just find something else to do. Having Dad flipping out would kind of throw my whole brain out of whack. I was always happily doing my business but then Dad would come and throw a wrench into my world.

When I was a kid, I lived two lives. One was fun and happy, playing hockey and with friends, working on the farm and working or playing at the racetrack. I even mostly enjoyed going to school.

Then there was life with Dad. It was always tense and scary from the earliest time I can remember. You never knew if or what he was going to flip out about.

When I was little, Dad never kept at me like he did with Jay. He treated the dogs and horses and cows much the same as he treated his close family. If we grovelled at his feet, he could kick us in the belly when he was in that mood. Then we would get a pat on the head. No animal on the farm lived without fear of Dad. You did not want to draw my dad's attention if you were in his family. I learned at a young age to stay away from him when I could.

If Dad was around, it was like a big dark cloud sucking the happiness out of you. You never knew what he was going to do. I always expected something crazy and violent, but you never knew what or when or to what magnitude it would be. Usually high, though. I can't think of any time when he was kind or sympathetic to his family without a spectator or witnesses around.

Whenever you had to ask Dad a question about the farm or the cattle, you made sure you had all of the questions in order and you might get a straight answer. You couldn't start a conversation with anyone else, or he would cut in and tell everybody what you were going to say. He wouldn't let you talk. Any conversation you had you could bet he was eavesdropping on. Mom and I could be having a conversation at the end of the hall, and he would yell out some detail.

Dad got progressively more violent with me from the time I was about 11 years old. I always tried to act tough, and I pretended to laugh everything off, but I was terrified a lot of the time. Even when people were around you had to be careful what you said, because he would wait and get even with you later if you said something he didn't like.

Many times I was scared to death when Dad was coming after me. There was no guessing where his rage would go if he got his hands on you. He often hit me or smashed me against things. That was bad enough, but when he truly flipped out, he was so scary I could barely move to get away. If you've ever had a nightmare where you're trying to run away from someone, and you're so terrified that your legs will barely work enough, that's what it felt like for me when Dad would snap into a rage and come after me.

Every time I got away from Dad, I felt shaky and weak, like I was going to be sick. I would stay hidden until I could see by his actions that he had cooled down. A few times I stayed out overnight. I kept a sleeping bag in an old cabin by our dugout. I'd wait until I saw him out in the open the next day, to see if he was still mad. The strange thing was, he'd always act like he had done nothing wrong. He would laugh about me running off and hiding from him. He'd say, "Are you done being an asshole now?"

The thing that was sure to send Dad into a rage was if you defied him, or even if you questioned him. I always made sure I had an escape route before working with him in an enclosed place. I did the same thing you do when you're working with cattle, where a cow might go berserk due to a past mishap, or a cow is giving birth. Or when you're working with heavy farm equipment that can crush you easily. When working with Dad, you tried to have a guaranteed getaway plan. You did not want to get trapped.

For a couple of years before my brain injury, Dad respected me. When I was shoeing horses, I was doing well and had a good name in the horse business, so he thought I was worthy. I was also quite strong, shoeing up to ten racing chuckwagon horses a day. Dad couldn't push me around, and he knew that, so he didn't try.

Nowadays, even if the horse is well behaved, I can barely put two shoes on a four-footed horse. I know I wouldn't be hired by a chuckwagon driver or a racehorse trainer. It is impossible to do high-quality work with hemiparesis, which is a form of paralysis to one side of your body.

After my accident, Dad was good for a year or so, when I couldn't think for myself at all. Then he started mocking me and making fun of me, always taunting me. I didn't realize at first what he was doing, but as I started to come back to reality, I could tell he was trying to lure me in. That way, he would have an excuse for coming after me if I said anything back. My dad was seventy-three years old, and he could still wipe the floor with me with one hand tied behind his back. Sometimes I told him I knew what he was doing, and that he should be ashamed of himself, but that didn't stop him. He only came at me more.

Every single day I dreaded having to deal with my dad. I never knew what he would come up with. He would flip out and attack me for any little thing. He was always mean.

The day I shot my dad started out lovely. I was so happy just getting back from my honeymoon the day before. Jenny and I had spent ten days travelling down to Vancouver Island and visiting our extended family. It was nothing but pleasant. I got none of the meanness I always lived with from Dad, and I felt relaxed. When you are living with craziness and fear all the time and it's like your normal way of life, you are always aware of the danger.

On that morning none of that was on my mind. I was just happy and excited to be moving along with my life. That's why it blindsided me when Dad went crazy and started after me. I had been away for two weeks with nonviolent people, and I didn't see it coming.

I was working with the bobcat moving sand I had found on one of our local gas leases. I put a little sand on a low spot on my house trailer's water well line. Dad had met me on the road on his quad to say I didn't need to go to the lease to get sand, because there was a pile of dirt where Mom was going to have her cement laid on the side of their house. I was halfway there though, so I decided to go and get a load of sand at the new dugout first. As I was headed down the gravel trail between Mom and Dad's house, I saw Dad again. He asked me to dump a couple five-gallon buckets of used oil into the fifty-gallon drum sitting beside the shop. "Sure," I said. I wasn't really sure why he asked me to do that, when he could do it easier than me.

After dumping the two buckets of oil, I climbed back into the bobcat and started moving dirt into the potholes on Mom and Dad's driveway. I saw Dad screaming at me from their house's deck, so I shut the bobcat off and asked him what was wrong.

"Don't be wasting that dirt there!" he yelled at me.

"Oooookay," I said to myself. I pulled away from the two or three potholes that were left and went back to the dirt pile. Mom and Dad's septic discharge would always pump out on the edge of their yard into the ditch. I decided that three loads of dirt would block it off nice and make the septic fluid discharge the other way, down to a culvert away from the house. After dumping two loads I almost ran over Dad, who was suddenly beside the bobcat.

"You son of a bitch. Always fucking around!" he screamed at me. He tried to reach into the bobcat and grab me from the side.

I turned the bobcat so he had to back away. I decided I would go and get the third load of dirt, dump it, then get outta there and go work somewhere else. When I was heading back, I saw Dad climbing up into the McCormick. I dumped the load, and then realized he was coming after me in the tractor. I quickly backed up onto the road and then started to drive away from him. The bobcat is a tortoise and the McCormick is a hare, so I was afraid I would get run over. I turned off the road and wheeled the bobcat in behind the harrows and climbed out.

Dad roared up and slammed the tractor into park, then jumped out and charged at me. I stumbled around the other way, keeping the harrows between him and me. The whole while, he was cursing my mom and grandma. I finally made a run for it over the culvert.

I can't run very fast, because my right leg is partially par-alyzed, and at first I thought he was going to catch me. When I started to get some distance on him, he started cursing at me, then yelled, "Come back! I just wanna talk to you!" A few times when I was young I stopped when he said, "I just wanna talk to you," and then Dad grabbed me and punched me out. I knew what he meant by it, and I was not going to let him catch me.

He finally quit chasing me. On my way to the shop, I was thinking about what would happen to Jenny and our new baby if Dad had flipped me over in the bobcat or caught me on the road. What would happen if he punched me in the head and messed up my brain again?

I decided I had to stand up to him. I remembered the time when Jay finally stood up to him, and Dad quit beating on Jay, and I thought maybe the same thing would work for me. But Jay is ten times stronger than me, and I knew I couldn't stand up to Dad without something that would make him back off.

I expected Dad to go to his and Mom's house for lunch, but I knew we were planning to go pick up stock waterers after that. I kept thinking about what I could do to keep him from getting his hands on me. I was sure with the rage Dad was in, he wasn't done with me yet. I thought about the three different waterers we had set up in the spring, and I could remember getting hit and chased at every separate place.

I knew if I pulled a knife out Dad would laugh at me. He would probably take it away and use it on me. I thought the 30-30 rifle would be too much. I decided my .22 Ruger pistol would be the thing to use. I'm not a very good shot. My mom and brother tease me about that. All I wanted it for was the scare factor.

Afterwards I could see that a gun could never have worked to make Dad respect me. But as I was running away from him that day, it seemed like a good idea. I thought I would just load the gun and keep it on me. When he came after me, I would pull it out and tell him to behave. I pictured in my mind that Dad would then think about it, realize what he was doing, and go, "Okay." Then we would get the work done and move on to the next job. He would respect me after that.

As I ran toward my shop, I could hear Dad driving the trac-tor. He was probably wrecking the work I just did. He had done that lots of times before. I finally got to my shop's southeast door, passing by my Ford Ranger. The Ford still had the keys in it, from where we had left it the day before. I thought of getting into it and driving away, but the work had to be done, and that would just delay the situation. Plus I wasn't sure where Dad was. He might be on the other side of the haystack. If he caught me trying to leave he could smash my truck with the tractor bucket or flip it over.

I went into my shop and closed the door behind me. I hurried to the cabinet that had the safe code written in it. There was no paper handy, so I wrote the code on my hand so I could remember it.

I opened the safe. The Ruger was sitting on the second shelf down, where I had put it a few months before, after it had taken me six or seven shots to kill a pig. I was disgusted by that and swore I would never use my pistol to slaughter an animal again. If I had to kill a pig, or any animal, I would use the 30-30 rifle.

As I was getting the pistol, I pictured myself pulling it out when Dad started flipping out and trying to grab me. I could hold it on him and tell him to leave me alone. I was a married man now with a child on the way. It was time for him to start treating me like a grown-up and quit attacking me.

By this time, I was fully back in my awareness about watching out for him. Even though I expected him to go back to his house for lunch, I listened for his quad. That was a rule around the farm. We always listened for him. You did not ever want to get cornered.

I planned to put ten bullets in the gun clip, put the clip in my pistol, then head for my house. I was busy putting bullets in the clip and didn't hear anything until Dad smashed my shop door open. I was shocked and terrified when he burst into my shop with the bright sunlight glaring behind him. All I could see was his shape coming through the doorway. He was screaming curses and threats at me. I was trapped. It was the worst thing that could happen.

"I've got a gun!" I yelled. I was scared to death. Dad never went anywhere without the quad, and he had snuck up on me.

"Bullshit!!! You little son of a bitch!!!" he yelled.

As he came rushing toward me, I jammed the clip into the

pistol with just three bullets in it. I lifted the pistol and pulled the trigger, thinking, *Stay away from me!* Nothing happened.

I brought the pistol down and tried pushing some buttons. Dad continued to curse and come toward me. I lifted the pistol again, pointing it in his direction. I knew I had to prove to him that I could defend myself. I pulled the trigger. Again, nothing happened.

I thought, *He will kill me now. He'll be so mad that I stood up to him. He'll catch me and beat me to death if he knows I can't get the gun to fire.* My brain was almost frozen with fear. All I could think was, *I have to get this gun to fire!*

I brought the pistol down again and must have switched the true safety off. My hands were sweaty. They were shaking so much I could hardly hold the gun.

I didn't really expect the gun to go off, since I'd tried twice already. But I had to try. I wasn't aiming at anything when I raised it up and pulled the trigger. I was aware that if it did go off, I didn't want to hit a window and break it. Everything happened at once. I raised the gun, looked up, and pulled the trigger. *Blam.* The pistol went off. It was like a falling tree when Dad fell.

He just wants me to think he has fainted or something, and I'll come up to him, and he'll grab me, I said to myself. Everything happened at fast speed. I stood back and watched him, waiting for him to get up.

When he didn't move, I walked up to him a few seconds later, with the gun still in my hand. I wasn't about to touch him or get too close in case he grabbed me. I knew he wasn't faking when I saw a trickle of blood running out of his nose. He was lying on his stomach with his head turned to his right. I couldn't see any other blood, but I was pretty sure he was dead, so I thought he might have had a heart attack.

All I could see burned into my eyes was the shape of him against the bright sunlight in the doorway, but he must have turned around, because that's how he landed. So that's what I told the cops. That he must have realized I was trying to fire the gun, and he was leaving.

I was stunned. I put the other two bullets back in the .22 bullet box and put the Ruger on the shelf before locking the safe. I tried to phone Mom, but she didn't answer. I tried to phone Jenny, but she didn't answer. *I better phone 911,* I thought to myself.

While I sat at the picnic table, still stunned, I thought about all the things Dad had done to Mom and Jay and me all our lives. Even though I was upset about what had happened, I was relieved that he was dead.

I thought he might have had a heart attack because I fired the gun. I knew it was more of an accident than anything that he was dead, because I never tried to kill my dad or hit him with a bullet. I simply wanted him to know that I could defend myself.

But when the police were questioning me later, they said to me it was all the same, that murder's murder. So I didn't think it mattered how Dad's death happened. It was all going to be the same result. I didn't tell them about my plan to get my gun and carry it with me to make Dad behave, because no one asked me about it. They had me hating on Dad because I was locked in jail for something he caused. I was mad at Dad, and I didn't care at the time if they thought I meant to kill him. By that time it was all so jumbled in my brain. I was so cold and so tired I didn't care what I said.

As we talked and worked together on his story, I could see the scenario play out as Mat described it, and feel the terror he'd experienced. I remembered trying to stand up to Sandy when he attacked me, before I'd learned that if I fought back it only made him worse. I remembered how my body and brain would shut down. How I'd be unable to think at all—frozen—and then finally telling him whatever he wanted to hear, whether it was true or not.

There was no doubt in my mind about what had happened, but I also realized that a judge and jury who didn't know Mat or Sandy could have doubts about the story. Revealing Sandy's character through the eyes of people not connected to Mat would be crucial.

CHAPTER 23

AS MAT'S LAWYER, Dave Cunningham had received copies of the police interrogation transcripts for Mat, Jason, and me, along with videotapes of the questioning Mat had undergone.

I was dismayed when I watched the films and read the transcripts after Mat was out on bail. Mat, Jason, and I had all said things that could be seen as highly incriminating toward Mat. There was no doubt the cops who had interrogated Mat were expert.

I tried to look at it from the law's angle: a twenty-seven-year-old killing a seventy-three-year-old with a bullet to the back. Without understanding Mat and the backstory, it must have seemed like an open-and-shut case.

On the afternoon of the shooting, the RCMP had requested that a charge of second-degree murder be laid. That was the original charge they told Mat he would be facing. I didn't have a clue at the time what the difference was among the various categories of murder: first-degree, second-degree, or manslaughter. I knew what self-defence was, though. Mat might have hit Sandy in the back of the neck, but I knew without a doubt that he had fired in self-defence. I could easily visualize Sandy crashing through the door, yelling at Mat. Mat being scared to death, because he had decided he was going to stand his ground. Sandy's anger when he saw that Mat had a gun. Sandy yelling at Mat and coming toward him. The gun failing to fire, Mat's brain overloading, and panic setting in. In the original police photographs of the scene, there was an axe lying at Sandy's feet. The axe was clearly visible in the photos. At some point, the situation changed and Sandy turned to leave, or to grab the axe. We'll never know for sure which it was.

In my view, what had happened was an accidental shooting,

brought on by Sandy's own actions. A terrible situation, but not an intentional murder.

At the time, I was disillusioned with the police for overreacting and, in my mind, deliberately misinterpreting the incident. I expected them to be unbiased. I know now that, regardless of the training members of law enforcement have, they are still human beings, with their own filters, biases, and agendas.

It wasn't only the axe lying by Sandy's feet that was overlooked or ignored. Some of the information in the disclosure—the evidence provided by the police—was incorrect. I was alarmed at the inaccuracies. The disclosure said that Mat and Sandy had gone after each other on their machines; in fact, Sandy had chased Mat with the four-wheel-drive tractor while Mat was on the bobcat trying to get away. The disclosure said that Mat had gone into his house to get the gun and had come back out with it. In fact, the gun was kept in a safe in Mat's shop, as he had told the police.

After more interrogation of Mat on Friday night, the chief Crown prosecutor was presented with further information, causing him to agree to up the charge against Mat to first-degree murder. Under duress, Mat had seemed to indicate he'd had enough of his father's violence and had consciously shot him for that reason.

At first I couldn't figure out how Mat could have been so naive. The decision to arm himself, thinking he could pull a gun on his father and get him to behave, wasn't logical. Maybe he'd thought it would work like in the old westerns, where the good guy pulls a gun and makes the bad guy smarten up. Then I remembered the time I'd tried to buy a gun from Sandy's friend Teddy. If I'd been desperate enough to consider using a gun to defend myself, how could I not understand Mat having the same reaction? There was nothing else that might equalize him with his father.

As part of Mat's defence, Dave Cunningham would have to clearly explain Mat's thought processes, both why he'd taken the gun out of the safe and why he'd said what he had to the police while being interrogated. In the weeks after Mat was released on bail, he and I went over things time and time again.

"What did you think would happen later in the day if you pulled a gun on your father and made him behave himself?"

I asked him. "Didn't you think about what he'd do to you first chance he got?"

"Right then, I never thought past getting the day's work done," Mat told me. "We were planning to go move the waterer after lunch, and I just wanted to get that done without Dad hitting me with something. I thought, I'm getting a gun, and when Dad starts flipping out on me, I'll pull it out and tell him to behave. I never heard him come to my shop. That's the last thing I expected. It was lunchtime, and I thought he'd probably go to your house for lunch. If he hadn't come into my shop after I got the gun loaded, I would have gone to my house and had lunch. I probably would have changed my mind and put the gun away after I thought about it. But I didn't get time to think."

"Why didn't you ever tell the cops flat out that you never meant to shoot him?" I asked.

"In my mind, I knew I never meant to shoot him," Mat said. "I was scared and all I wanted was to get a shot off so he'd see I could defend myself. Then I couldn't get my gun to work, and that scared me even more. Every time I tried to organize my thoughts and say that to the cops, they would cut me off and go in a different direction. I finally gave up trying to think before I answered them."

"What about when you said to the cops, 'That's when I knew. Enough's enough.' Why in the world would you say that?" I asked him.

"As I was running, after I got away from Dad, I thought about getting the gun. I thought, *Enough's enough, I'm getting a gun and making him behave.* I wanted the cops to let me go back home, so I was trying to give them the best answers I could. I got confused from all of the talking in circles. They kept asking me the same thing. Then I thought, *It doesn't matter what happens now anyway. Everybody is safe.* Dad could never hurt you or any of us again.

"Everything happened so fast. I was panicking because I couldn't get the gun to fire. I was looking down at the gun, pushing buttons. Dad was screaming and coming at me. I was cornered. Then I looked up and pulled the trigger at the same time. The gun fired. I had never even aimed. I was thinking of the shit I would be in if I shot out a window. And then he fell.

"The cops said they wanted to understand my side of the story. They obviously knew I was brain damaged. I was pretty sure they were trying to help me. When I said to them, 'It was decided,' I meant I had decided I was going to protect myself with something I could stand up to Dad with. I decided I was not going to run away like I had a hundred times before when Dad attacked me. I hoped that when the gun went off, Dad would go, 'Oh. He's serious, I better smarten up.' And then the gun went off and he fell over."

"What about when the one cop said, 'What were you aiming at?' And you said, 'At my dad, I guess.' Why did you say that?" I asked.

"That's what I hit, so I guess obviously that's where my gun was pointing. At other times when they asked me the same question, I said, 'In the area.' My brain was scrambled. I thought, *The cops are supposed to be on the good guy's side*, so I tried to tell them the truth."

Jason, Jenny, and I were fully aware that when he was under pressure, Mat could make unwise choices and say unfitting things. But we also knew that he was incapable of deceit and didn't have a violent bone in his body. I didn't blame the homicide police for not knowing that. How could they? They formed their own opinion of what had happened and why, then set out to fill in the blanks. If I'd watched the same story play out on my favourite cop show, *Law and Order*, I would have been rooting for the cops all the way. Because, like Matti, I'd thought the cops were always on the side of the good guy. Through Matti's ordeal, I learned that police officers are normal human beings, as prone to weakness and error as the rest of us. The fact that they go through training and wear uniforms doesn't take away their personalities or change their characters.

Mat was mentally overpowered by the cops who were interrogating him. Rather than realize where they were leading him, he'd kept following along. He thought, since he knew what had happened, they'd be able to figure it out too.

I was determined to find a way we could explain the working of Mat's brain in court. I turned, for the thousandth time, to the internet, finding some excellent articles by experts in the field that helped to explain what makes some brain-injured people

more gullible. I passed the information along to Dave Cunningham. I also learned through my reading that people with mental
disabilities often falsely confess to crimes under questioning
because they are tempted to accommodate and agree with
authority figures. Despite that, few law enforcement interrogators
are given any special training on questioning suspects with mental disabilities. I hoped that information would work in Matti's
favour, too.

CHAPTER 24

ONCE MAT WAS home, easily following his bail conditions of not going over a hundred kilometres from home, not drinking alcohol, being in the house by 11 p.m., phoning his parole officer twice a week, and not having any firearms, life returned to a semblance of normal. Although the immensity of what Mat was facing never went away, there were times that fall when we got so busy around the farm it wasn't the foremost thing on my mind. Then I'd get an e-mail or call from Roy Carter or Dave Cunningham, jolting me back to the reality of our situation.

As well, my mind was still in turmoil about Sandy being a pedophile. The terrible stories I'd heard from the women he'd abused as young girls played over and over in my head.

I didn't have nightmares, exactly, because I never really slept. I would doze, then wake up with disturbing thoughts still vivid in my mind. I'd always been able to give myself a shake and deal with what life had thrown my way, but I was sinking this time. Sandy had put himself out there as a model citizen, a larger-than-life good guy. I thought of the many times he had come home and told me someone had complimented him on how wonderful he was for looking after his disabled wife and son. Each time, I had said to myself, *If only they knew the truth about what you're really like.* Now I realized I'd been far from knowing the full truth myself. I couldn't get my head around how he'd managed to keep his secrets hidden from me for nearly thirty years. I forced myself to carry on, because the farm needed to function, and so did we. If I fell apart it would be a disaster. But I was spinning more and more, never getting enough sleep and rarely being able to clear my mind. My thoughts sickened me.

In early February 2011, I learned that Peter Nilsson, who had coached Jason's midget hockey team fifteen years before, had injured his eye in a furnace explosion. When I phoned to see how he was doing, Peter's response surprised me.

"Oh, I'm really good," he told me.

"Right on. So your eye is okay, then?"

"Oh, no, I can barely see out of it."

"Then how can you say you're really good? I know your knees are messed up. Now you're blind in one eye. That doesn't sound good to me."

"It's all in how you view what happens to you," he replied, in a mellow voice. "This must have happened to teach me something."

The conversation did not fit with the man I remembered. Peter was a large, aggressive, volatile, athletic fellow. He thought nothing of jumping off the bench and confronting the opposing team to defend the rowdy teenage boys he coached, and they loved and admired him. Other than Jason and a few local boys, Peter's team had consisted largely of misfits from Grande Prairie, kids who'd been banned from other teams because they couldn't conform. Peter had molded that motley group into league winners.

I thought Peter must be pulling my leg with this new, warm fuzzy attitude. "I don't believe things happen for any reason," I said. "I think shit happens and you deal with it. There's not a purpose in any of it."

When Peter mentioned he was studying to be a shaman, I laughed. I pictured a witch doctor shaking a rattle and going into a trance. I'm a skeptical person, and visualizing Peter as a shaman was ridiculous. I got off the phone, still thinking he must be kidding. Over the next few days, however, something he'd said during our discussion about clearing your mind of negative stuff kept niggling at me. My brain was so full of negative stuff it felt like I was about to explode. I called Peter and asked if he thought he could help me.

"If you want me to, I can," he said.

"I want you to."

We made arrangements for him to come over to my house.

⇢

Fear, guilt, and anger. Those are the three main emotions that cause people to become mired in negative energy, Peter told me at the onset of our session. The first step in overcoming them, he said, is to recognize those emotions for what they are. It's important to let the past go and not be too attached to the future.

I went on the offensive immediately. "There's no way I can let the past go. I'm spending all my time trying to put together a picture of what Sandy was like, reliving the hell he put me and so many other people through. And the future! How in the world can I not be attached to the future when my youngest son is facing life in prison for killing his father?"

Peter waited for me to cool down a bit. He wasn't making excuses for Sandy, he assured me, or saying what had happened didn't matter. What he meant was that I wouldn't do myself or Matti any good by letting those emotions drag me down. It was important to separate the fact-finding components of what I was doing from the negative emotions the search was provoking. "You can take something good from everything that happens," Peter said, "even if it's a terrible thing. It can be used as a learning experience."

I protested some more, but after a while I could see some sense in what he was saying.

I needed to stay in the moment, Peter advised me, focus my energy on what I was doing now rather than obsessing about things I had no control over. There were so many decisions to be made, and angles to be considered. It felt like I was being pulled in a dozen directions at once, and any wrong decision could drastically affect the rest of my life and the lives of those close to me.

Peter handed me a thin six-sided crystal, about two inches long and wider at one end than the other. "If you believe in this," he said, "it will work for you. I want you to focus on blowing your negative energy into this crystal. Just hold it up to your lips and concentrate on removing that energy from yourself."

Once the negative energy was gone, Peter explained, it would be up to me to recognize those feelings when they started again and to block them. I'd need to work at keeping them away.

I felt too awkward to try the crystal with Peter there, but no sooner was he out the door than I was blowing into it. The first time, nothing happened to change the constant feeling that my guts were being put through a grinder. I decided I had to quit being skeptical; otherwise the crystal was guaranteed to not work. I sat quietly and focussed my thoughts. Once I was aware of the horrible feelings I carried inside me, I closed my eyes and blew softly into the crystal. I blew again and again.

When I stopped blowing, for the first time in months my stomach wasn't burning. It felt strangely hollow. I stayed still for a bit, then moved around the room in my wheelchair. My mind suddenly flooded like a Technicolor movie, filled with torturous thoughts of Sandy and what he had done. The burning in my stomach came back. I took out the crystal and softly blew my thoughts into it, with the intention of removing them from my body. The fear and burning vanished once again.

From then on, I carried the crystal with me and used it whenever I felt overwhelmed. I knew it was all some sort of head game, but it worked for me.

⁂

A few weeks later, Dave Cunningham called to say the dates in Mat's trial had been set. I sent an e-mail out to our friends and supporters to let them know.

Dear Friends,

We have the dates for Mat's trials. In one way I'm glad, and in another way it's unsettling.

The preliminary is May 9, 2011, booked for a week. In the preliminary, the Crown has to satisfy a judge that a jury might convict on the charges that are laid (first-degree murder). If the judge doesn't believe that could happen, he/she then lowers the charge.

The next and last stage of the process is a jury trial starting November 28, booked for two weeks.

Mat has been home since last October 26. He has certain bail conditions he has to meet, but it's easy for him to do. He's VERY happy with where he's at.

Jenny, Mat's wife, is due to have her baby on April 9. We're all getting excited about having a happy event around here.

I'd like to reiterate how very much we all appreciate your support with Mat's bail, and the moral support we've received. We're doing well and fine, and it's largely due to all of you.

Holly

CHAPTER 25

WITH ALL THE stress Jenny was going through, both her mom and I worried about her pregnancy. While Mat was in jail, Jenny and I had spent many evenings talking. I knew how important this baby was to her. I figured that if Matti had to go to prison, Jenny would hold it together for their baby.

As her due date neared, Jenny had issues with erratic blood pressure and she was admitted to hospital nearly two weeks early. When her blood pressure wouldn't settle down, her doctor decided to induce labour.

Mat and Jenny had a deal that Jenny would name the baby if it was a girl, and Mat would name a boy. Percy was Mat's name of choice for two reasons: it wasn't a common name, and a good friend and well-respected farmer, Percy Head, lived just across the muskeg from us. Mat thought Percy would be a good solid name for a boy to live up to.

Mat, and Jenny's mom, Judy, planned to be in the room with Jenny for the delivery. The rest of us—a group of Jenny's friends, her twin sister, her niece, her father, and I—hung about in the waiting room. The doctor stopped in to tell us it would be at least a couple of hours before the birth, so Jenny's dad and I went down to the cafeteria for a bite to eat. We were just getting settled over our soup and sandwiches, when we heard the intercom buzz. An alarm pinged shrilly, and a voice called, "Code Pink. Code Pink. Labour and Delivery. Stat. Code Pink. Labour and Delivery. Stat."

I'd heard those alarms ping dozens of times while I waited in the atrium outside the brain trauma ICU at Edmonton's University Hospital after Mat's accident. It was never a good thing. I knew what we were hearing now was bad, and I knew it was about Jenny. Denis and I left our food on the table and rushed toward the elevators.

The Labour and Delivery floor was a beehive of activity centred on the room Jenny was in. We were asked to stay in the waiting room so we didn't clutter the hallway. My mind spun as I sat in my wheelchair, leaning my head against the wall. Fear gripped my heart.

We finally learned that Percy had been facing downward when Jenny began pushing. The doctor managed to flip him into the proper position, only to have him flip downward again just as Jenny pushed. The baby became lodged. The umbilical cord was pinched, cutting off his oxygen. There was no time for a Caesarean section. The doctors had to yank him out as quickly as possible. They hurried desperately, but it all took time. When they finally got Percy delivered, he didn't breathe or have a heartbeat for the next twelve minutes.

Percy's condition was extremely critical, and when they finally got him breathing, he was rushed to the Neonatal Intensive Care Unit. Percy had had multiple seizures because of oxygen deprivation. He was being treated with anti-seizure medication, and he'd been sedated to keep him as quiet as possible. When a newborn brain is oxygen-starved, cell death doesn't occur instantly. Hypothermia, or cooling, therapy has made what was previously an impossible situation treatable. The therapy prevents the baby's brain from swelling and prevents cell death from chemical reactions, which happen when pH levels fall too low and the blood becomes acidic.

While Jenny was taken to surgery to repair damage that had occurred during the birth, Matti and I went up to be with Percy. We were allowed to touch him lightly, once, with our fingertips. The hospital had already begun the cooling process, and any contact that would warm him was disallowed. It was distressing to see a little newborn baby lying completely exposed and still, his body bloated from the trauma of his birth.

Jenny arrived while Mat and I were waiting beside Percy, pushed in a hospital wheelchair by a nurse. She was determined to see her baby before he was flown to the hospital in Edmonton. I backed my wheelchair away so Mat and Jenny could both be close to their son. I watched as they gazed at him, knowing they wanted more than anything to hold him. Jenny reached out and quickly touched Percy's cold little finger.

An air ambulance crew was readying all the equipment needed to keep Percy alive on the flight to Edmonton. As soon as they got the go-ahead, they put him in a tiny incubator on a gurney and rolled him out the door. I was full of fear at the thought of what Mat and Jenny might be facing. Their faces were suffused with love for their baby, however—a humbling and necessary thing for me to see. I accepted, once again, that we would all have to pull together and do whatever it took to get over this new bump in the road.

Mat had been given permission to attend Jenny's delivery, but his bail conditions didn't allow him to go anywhere else. When I phoned Dave Cunningham and told him the situation, he said immediately, "Tell them to head for Edmonton. I'll deal with Mat's bail conditions."

Once again the community was there to help. Rocky McAusland from the Grovedale Old Stars Hockey Club handed Mat and Jenny an envelope of money to help with expenses. Community members dropped off donations at the two Grovedale convenience stores, and the local volunteer fire department gave them money too. Mat and Jenny packed some clothes quickly and headed for Edmonton.

They were thankful to get a room at the Ronald McDonald House in Edmonton while Percy was in Stollery Children's Hospital. For the first three days, he was kept sedated and partially wrapped in a rubbery blanket with coolant running through it. After that, he was slowly warmed to body temperature, and then given food, a few drops at a time through a nasogastric tube to his stomach. Percy's shoulder had been wrenched during birth, and there was some concern there might be lasting damage, but that seemed a minor consideration compared to the larger battle he was fighting.

The baby forged steadily ahead and, after eight days, he was transferred back to the Queen Elizabeth II Hospital in Grande Prairie. Jenny was able to stay in the hospital with him this time, until they were finally able to take him home. The doctors didn't sugar-coat anything. We all knew there was a very strong chance Percy would be disabled, possibly with cerebral palsy.

Percy's pediatrician, Dr. Faltaous, informed Jenny at a follow-up appointment that Percy had been the first baby in the

Grande Prairie hospital to have the cooling procedure initiated. The staff at the QEII had received training for the procedure just two weeks prior to his birth. Miracles do sometimes happen.

As the months passed, and Percy continued reaching the normal milestones for a child his age, we were profoundly grateful. Against all the odds, he has never shown any ill effects from his birth.

CHAPTER **26**

OVER THE WINTER and the spring that followed, Mat, Jenny, and I had numerous meetings with Dave Cunningham and Roy Carter. Since Dave's small office in Grande Prairie was up a flight of stairs, and not at all wheelchair accessible, Roy and Allana had graciously offered us the use of office space at their business for our meetings. Roy, Dave, and I had traded more than five hundred e-mail messages by the time of Mat's preliminary hearing in May.

Life went on in a somewhat normal fashion at the farm. We no longer had our cows, but we lambed 150 ewes between mid-March to mid-April. Since she was pregnant, Jenny hadn't been allowed to be around the ewes that were lambing. Mat and Laurie did the outside chores. I stayed inside and warmed chilled lambs in the kitchen sink, then tubed colostrum into them to give them a kick-start. Lambing is an intense time, because the young are born night and day, usually two or more per ewe. The newborns often need a bit of assistance getting warmed up and started on nursing. We were busy and sleep-deprived. As always, I loved the farm work, but almost every time I checked my e-mail there was something to pull my mind back to the charges against Mat.

Dr. Daniel Senekal, a good friend of Roy's and a highly respected ophthalmologist, heard of Mat's plight, and he offered, free of charge, to do extensive visual testing on Mat, in order to explain to the jury how Mat sees. In anticipation of being an expert witness at Mat's trial in December, Dr. Senekal even postponed a trip he had planned to visit his ailing father in South Africa.

Dr. Senekal's formal report on Mat's vision restrictions would turn out to be a critical element in Mat's defence. After testing Mat, he was able to document how the blind area in Mat's field of vision, and the inability of Mat's eyes to adjust quickly from bright to dim lighting, would have severely affected Mat's perception of where Sandy was and which direction he was facing. What Mat would have seen was shadowy, with the area from one to three o'clock in his field of vision completely blacked out.

From the first time we'd met at Roy and Allana Carter's place in September, Dave Cunningham had cautioned us that we must put TV shows like *Law and Order* out of our minds. A lot of what was portrayed on the shows had no application to Canadian law, he informed us. In the months that followed, my main source of education was the internet: I was constantly searching for information about what to expect and how the Canadian legal system works. Until Mat was charged, I hadn't even realized there was a difference between criminal law and civil law. I'd climbed a long way on the learning curve, but I was dismayed to learn from Dave that it was not true, as I had believed, that if Mat were not convicted of first-degree murder, he would be free to go.

Instead, Dave informed me, Mat would start off facing the maximum charge, and work his way down the ladder. If a jury decided that he hadn't carried out a planned and premeditated murder, but had intended to kill his father when he pulled the trigger, he could still be sentenced for second-degree murder. A first-degree murder conviction meant a sentence of twenty-five years to life in prison, Dave told us. Conviction for second-degree murder meant a sentence of ten to twenty-five years, also in a maximum-security prison.

Although the Crown prosecutors were diligent in presenting the Crown's case at Mat's preliminary hearing, I got the sense they were not antagonistic toward him as they had been at his bail hearing. I knew, though, that regardless of any feelings they might have, it was their job to convince a judge and jury to uphold the charges against Mat.

Various RCMP officers, along with the homicide cops who had originally interrogated Mat, took the stand to state why they felt he should be convicted of first-degree murder. The Crown raised a number of cases in which first-degree murder charges had been upheld by a court of law, citing the circumstances in each instance. From where I was sitting, there was no comparison to Matti's case in anything the Crown presented. In the end, however, the judge ruled that the first-degree murder charge would stand. The Crown had argued that as Mat was running to his shop, he had time to make a plan to kill his father, and the judge conceded that point.

Dave Cunningham had no visible reaction to the ruling. Perhaps to him the ruling wasn't a surprise, or maybe it was just his poker face at play. However, I was shocked to the core at the first-degree murder charge being allowed to stand. My head was spinning as I turned to leave.

As I wheeled toward the exit door, one of the constables who had interrogated Mat came toward me with a big smile. "Don't worry," he said. "Things will turn out all right."

Gratitude rushed through me. *He must know something we don't know*, I thought. *Oh my god, everything is going to be okay. Why would he say that if it wasn't true?*

A number of Sandy's siblings, along with some of our local friends and Jenny's family, were waiting for me outside the court-room. We were all in a state of shock at the judge's ruling. But the more I thought about what the constable had said, the better I felt. I was floating on a happy little cloud by the time I talked to Roy Carter later in the day. "You'll never believe this," I said gleefully, "That officer told me not to worry. He must know something we don't."

Instantly enraged, Roy spat out, "Don't you ever trust him!"

My stomach clenched as I remembered what I'd seen on the videotaped disclosure. I'd watched the police lie to Mat, manip-ulating him into saying what they wanted to hear. I'd watched Mat try to please them. For some reason that constable had decided to do the same thing with me, reassuring me everything would be all right while he was busy trying to put my son in a maximum-security prison for the rest of his life. He was playing a game that I was not equipped to understand.

After the preliminary hearing, the Crown prosecutor sug-gested to Dave Cunningham that the Crown might be agree-able to a plea of manslaughter. We were determined, however, that Mat should stick with self-defence. It seemed inconceivable that a jury of reasonable people would ever believe that he had planned what happened, or that he had intended to kill Sandy.

I continued to submit any information I gathered to Dave, and he processed it along with medical reports and other data he was collecting. We had eight months until the trial, and Dave was confident that Mat had a very strong case.

As the weeks rolled by, however, Dave became more and more concerned about what Mat might say on the stand. He'd already seen numerous examples of how, without grasping what was happening, Mat could easily be coerced and led to say almost anything. Jenny, Mat, and I spoke with Dave many times. We knew what the stakes were, and we wanted to stay the course in proving Mat innocent of any intentional wrongdoing. But the results of the preliminary trial had frightened us terribly. I worried that there might be some legal glitch or precedent that forced the judge and jury to convict Mat, even if they didn't believe he had intentionally done anything wrong. What if one of the jurors was a wife beater or pedophile who sympathized with Sandy?

As a jockey I'd ridden many racehorses that were tagged as "sure bets." Some of them had gone off the board as strong favourites but hadn't won the race. I'd been outrun on enough favourites to know there's no such thing as a "sure" thing.

As the trial date neared, Dave called from Edmonton to ask if we could set up a conference call. Mat, Jenny, and I gathered in my office, and I put my cordless phone on speaker mode.

Dave laid out the issue right away. "Mat, you have a decision to make. You need to decide if you want to accept the Crown's plea offer, or go to trial."

My instinct and strong desire was to continue to trial. I couldn't imagine a jury not understanding what had happened once they heard all the facts. But it wasn't my choice to make. I assured Mat and Jenny I'd support them whatever they decided.

I couldn't imagine a young couple having a tougher decision to make. I knew Mat and Jenny both wanted to go to trial, but the risk was just too great. If something went wrong at trial, it could be catastrophic. We knew the worst-case scenario was twenty-five years in a maximum-security prison—effectively, the end of Mat's life. Jenny told Mat she would stand behind him, whichever way he went, so the choice was now Mat's alone. My office was silent as we waited for his decision.

Within a few minutes, Mat said he had decided to accept the offer, and negotiate with the Crown. The Crown prosecutors by this time had obviously understood what had really happened. They were no longer portraying Mat as a heinous criminal, but they would still have the duty to prosecute him if he went to trial.

CHAPTER 27

OVER THE NEXT few weeks, Dave Cunningham prepared the defence's documentation regarding a plea bargain for the Crown prosecutors, and began the negotiations.

⊰◈⊱

Dear Madam/Sir:
Re: R. v. Matthew Gordon CRICHTON Section 235(1) C.C.

Further to my telephone conversations with Ms. Sihra, I enclose various materials designed to address the issues of the violent nature of the Deceased as well as the intent of the Accused. I must say that I have some misgivings in supplying this information because it amounts to disclosure of a substantial portion of the Defence case. I do so, however, because I accept in good faith Ms. Sihra's representation that this information is necessary for the Crown to consider whether a plea to criminal negligence (which would not attract a four-year minimum) would be acceptable. I must, however, insist on the following trust conditions: the enclosed are not to be used for the purpose of briefing witnesses nor are they to form the basis for cross-examination should no agreement as to plea be reached.

JEREMY HUSSEY WILL SAY:
I have been friends with Matthew Crichton since childhood.

As a young boy I spent many days over at the Crichtons as my mother helped break and train racehorses for them. I worked for the Crichtons for a few summers as a farm hand. I worked with Sandy and Mat almost every day those summers, and there were a few days where Sandy's temper got the best of him.

I got very afraid even if he wasn't yelling at me. There is one day in particular that stands out to me now, even as an adult.

One morning I was picked up by Sandy or Matthew, I don't remember which one, but we were fencing at the end of one of the fields. Right from the time I got there in the morning, Sandy was on Mat's case about anything he could.

It got worse throughout the day as Sandy kept threatening Mat. At the end of the day I thought we had made it through the day without disaster. We went to start the van that was taken out to the end of the field, and somehow the battery went dead. So, as we were boosting it, Sandy was bellowing directions at us. We didn't quite hear what he was saying, and we both had a confused sign because we weren't sure what he meant.

He came storming over to the van and lost it. Mat and I started to run through the field hiding behind the bales, running toward the house as Sandy came after us in the van. Eventually I stopped running and hid by one of the bales as Mat kept running. Sandy stopped the van and told me to get in. I did. I was afraid as I got in the van and sat at the very back as far away from Sandy as I could.

He continued to chase Mat through the field with me in the vehicle. When we got back to the house he was still boiling mad. He stopped the van and I got out and went into the house shocked and afraid. Mat continued to run and went to hide somewhere until Sandy cooled down. I was driven home shortly after that. I don't remember who drove me home that day.

PETER MCCULLOUGH WILL SAY:
As a summer job I found an occupation as a farm hand. This job required the operation of tractors, handling livestock, fence repairs and/or buildings. Many tasks on a farm are done daily. I was employed by Sandy Crichton and Holly Crichton, Crichton Farms. While employed I got the chance to work with a friend, Matthew Crichton. We did almost everything as a team and/or watched the other do it safely. On one occasion I recall, Matthew and I were asked by Sandy Crichton to do something in the field south of the house. So long ago, I don't exactly recall: perhaps it was to go get two tractors at the far end of the field and bring them to the house.

However, Matthew and I began walking to the field, we just left the house from lunch. There were bales in the field. The wind was blowing from the south to the north. We looked back and noticed Sandy Crichton going wild waving his arms, but due to the wind, we heard nothing. I could see his head was as red as a tomato. I asked Matthew if he knew what he meant. Matthew had no clue. I hollered back, not knowing if my voice would carry or not, "We can't hear you!" and we started walking back. Next thing he got in the old blue Ford and came towards us. I asked Matthew, "Is he gonna hit us?" [but] Matthew didn't respond. I turned and looked. Matthew was running. I ran with him behind a hay bale, and good thing, the truck came sliding by the hay bale, maybe a foot from us, and the bumper just missed the bale.

Matthew instructed me to run to the fence and make for the bush. I was scared but confused as the truck came past us again. You could see the fury and anger in Sandy Crichton's eyes while he was swearing. You could see it was directed at Matthew. I was worried. I told Matthew to run and he did. When the truck came towards us again, I stepped out with my hands up. Sandy came sliding up in a dust storm and yelled, "Get in!" I responded, "Hell no. You're crazy!" He insisted I get in because Matthew was getting away. I looked and he was in cover so I got in. Sandy was swearing how dumb we were and how bad Matthew was going to get it. I was ready to protect Matthew. We pulled up to the two bales Matthew was barricaded with and Sandy got out. He walked around the truck waving a stick from the truck box, saying "Get the f--k in that truck." Matthew got in the back seat and sat right behind me. It was a two-door Ford, extended cab. I was in the passenger front seat. Sandy got in, leaned over, pushed me against the door to prop himself with his left arm, and began beating Matthew with his right arm. Matthew was cornered, getting thudded. I could feel how hard he was hitting Matthew. He began crying.

Sandy took me home with Matthew in the back seat. We only joked of this incident later, too scared of the man to do anything. What sort of beating Matthew got after, I have no idea. Why the man snapped, we never knew. Matthew done nothing wrong that morning or the day before, but Sandy always seemed to have it out for Matthew. Had it out meaning, cause pain to, yell, scream, insult, disempower, humiliate.

WILFRID NILSSON WILL SAY:

In 1974, when I was sixteen, I worked for Sandy Crichton for six weeks, helping with farm work and haying.

My parents lived in Grovedale and were good friends with Sandy. He often came to their place visiting and I really liked him. Sandy offered me a job for the summer. My family was planning to move to Valleyview so my dad dropped me off at Sandy's farm, planning for them to move while I was working for Sandy. I was there for six weeks. I remember Sandy hitting Mary twice while I was there. One time was because we came in for lunch and it wasn't ready yet. He walked up to her and slapped her hard across the face. Sandy was a very powerful man.

The other time I saw him hit Mary I could see no reason for it whatsoever. He just strutted up to her and belted her across the face. The memory I have that has never left me is the oddness of how she never even said anything to him, before or after the blow, and how she just started sobbing and went to the bedroom. I really liked Mary; in fact, she changed what my perception of Natives had been up to that time. She was very intelligent, kind, and was a great cook. Sandy was very, very mean to her for no reason at all.

Another incident that made a huge impression on me was him beating a horse with a hammer. The horse was misbehaving and Sandy went wild with a hammer. He struck the horse five or six blows with it. The horse then stood quivering as he finished what he was doing with it. I remember thinking at the time that it was crazy how he would hit the horse so hard, when it was one of his best racehorses and was hopefully going to make him money.

One day Sandy and I came in for lunch from working in the field. There was a washbasin set up where we both washed up, then went and sat down for lunch. Sandy looked over at me across the table, jumped up and grabbed me by the hair. (I was 5'11" and about 130 lbs.) He dragged me over to the washbasin, shouting at me, "You better learn how to wash your face if you want to sit at the table with me!" as he was shoving my face in the basin. I couldn't believe how strong he was. I felt like a little child or a baby the way he dragged me by the hair, almost lifting me off the ground.

I was very scared of Sandy and extremely uncomfortable being there, but I had no way of leaving until my dad was coming for me. The things I remembered most about that summer were Sandy's intense meanness, and Mary's kindness and good cooking. When I got to Valleyview where my family had moved I started taking a self-defence course. I took it for two years. I made up my mind after that summer that I would never, ever strike a woman, and that I would learn to defend myself.

My parents stopped their friendship and never had any more to do with Sandy after that summer.

HOLLY CRICHTON

Sandy's wife, Mat's mother. Confined to a wheelchair since a riding accident in 1996. Holly can provide an extensive, almost endless narrative of abuse of herself and her sons at the hands of Sandy Crichton. She left him for extended periods twice, but returned because of her concern for her children and her dependency resulting from her disabilities. Several times she resorted to women's shelters. She, Jason and Mat attended a self-esteem workshop in an attempt to provide them with more resources to deal with Sandy. Holly believed that Sandy would one day kill her and she journalled numerous incidents of his abuse. She also recorded (audio) one or two incidents. Those tapes are in my possession. Holly is of the view that as bad as his behaviour had been historically it was escalating, particularly with respect to his most vulnerable target, Mat. Not more than two weeks prior to his death, Sandy terrified Holly so badly that she took refuge by locking herself in the elevator shaft in her residence until he went away. I asked Holly to restrict herself for these purposes to a few instances involving Mat which were subsequent to his injury:

—2008

Sitting at the table one day, Sandy started belittling Mat about how he was never going to amount to anything if he didn't start acting like a man. Mat had just put the dishes away for me and was having a coffee and reading a *National Geographic* magazine.

Mat just ignored Sandy and kept reading. Sandy kept trying different approaches to get a rise out of Mat, which he continued to ignore.

I finally couldn't stand it anymore and said: "What are you so insecure about that you can't stand to see your son have some consideration for other people?"

I wouldn't say he was yelling, but he was very loud. "Do I look like I'm talking to you? I'm talking to the retard here. At least he acts like a retard. Blame the brain injury all the time, but that's just an excuse."

Sandy started heckling him and trying to make Mat respond. Mat continued to look at his magazine and not look at Sandy. He finally belted Mat across the head. He yelled, "I'm talking to you. You look at me when I'm talking!"

Mat's magazine went flying. He sat and looked up at Sandy, not saying a word.

I said to Sandy, "You make me sick. What is it in you that makes you have to do these things?"

He mocked me like a little kid. "You make me sick, what is it in you that makes you have to do these things?" Then in a direct, angry voice he said to me, "*You* make *me* sick. You've turned Mat into a useless little pussy, just because you got everything you wanted when you were a kid."

He got up, went and sat in his La-Z-Boy recliner and turned the TV on.

—Summer 2008

We were putting up some fence panels behind a grain bin, Mat, Sandy, and I. Of course I was just giving directions as to whether they were lined up or not, because I couldn't physically help. Sandy was in our tractor with a grapple loader on the front of it. He would lower the bucket. Mat would hook the chain hanging from the bucket onto a panel so Sandy could pick up the panels to move.

Sandy was trying to tell Mat something. He was yelling and waving his arms around. Mat wasn't getting what he wanted. He got more and more agitated and was revving the motor and gesturing, but Mat still didn't get it. Finally Mat yelled at him to "Shut up!"

Sandy lurched the tractor at Mat. He ran into the back of the grain bin with the grapple loader. All he was thinking of was hitting Mat. He smashed the roof and side of the grain bin with his charge at Mat. Had the grapple not been low enough to hit the grain bin first, he would have pinned Mat against the bin with the tractor and crushed him.

—Summer 2009

Mat, Sandy, and I were having lunch and the floor was particularly dirty. I'd been busy and hadn't found time to sweep. As I was clearing the dishes up and putting lunch leftovers away, Mat grabbed the broom and started sweeping the floor. Sandy was reading a magazine at the table. He said to Mat, "That's woman's work, leave it alone!" Mat continued to sweep the floor and never said anything. Sandy got up from the table and said, "Let's go, Bud."

Mat continued to sweep, and Sandy started taunting him, calling him "Momma's little suckie boy," saying, "Your mother doesn't do anything else around here, so leave that alone."

Mat finally retorted, "Why do you have to be so ignorant?" Sandy rushed up to where Mat was standing by the fridge and started yelling, "You fucking little pussy… you'll never amount to anything."

He grabbed Mat's head and bounced it off the fridge. Mat almost fell down but managed to keep his feet. He held the broom up as if he was going to jab Sandy with it. Sandy taunted him more, "Go ahead, big man, try your luck!" He smirked at Mat and held his hands out to the side, with his fists clenched in a fighting stance.

Without saying another word Mat stopped sweeping the floor and went out to work with his father.

—2009

Sandy asked Mat to come and help him take the hood off the tractor so he could work on something in the motor. They went out to work, and it was all quiet for about an hour. I was outside with my dogs and could hear Sandy yelling, so I went over by the shop to see what was going on. I saw him screaming at Mat as Mat was trying to hold the hood in a certain way for it to go back into place.

I know Mat has trouble with balancing and holding stuff at the same time. I could see why he was having difficulty. Sandy rushed over and grabbed Mat by the back of the jacket. He flung

Mat aside and Mat hit the metal steps of the tractor. Sandy then mashed Mat's head against the tractor, screaming at him, "You never even tried to hold it right. You do stuff like that on purpose just to make me mad!"

—2010

Mat and Sandy were working on the disc-bine (which is used for cutting hay), changing some blades in it. Mat was lying on the ground trying to put nuts on bolts that Sandy was passing through from the top. For some reason he was having trouble getting the nuts started threading. Sandy was getting impatient and angry. I could hear him yelling at Mat. He was getting louder and louder. I was in the house and could hear him with the doors closed.

I went out on the deck to see what was going on. I saw Mat trying to scramble up from under the disc-bine. Sandy put his foot on Mat when Mat was partway out and gave him a hard shove. It sent Mat flying back underneath, and he crashed into the axle on the other side. Mat then scrambled out from under the front and got his distance from Sandy.

The yelling continued, and Mat started limping away. Sandy yelled at him, "Sure, make the farm suffer just because you're an ignorant little bastard. I can't do this work myself. You get back here and help me!"

Mat yelled at him to shove it, and Sandy charged at Mat, which caused Mat to speed up and keep out of his reach. Sandy went back to the disc-bine, reached down and grabbed a wrench to throw. When he realized Mat was too far away for him to hit, he dropped the wrench to the ground. He walked to the house, sat in his recliner and watched TV. Mat went back and put the disc-bine together by himself.

INTENTION

Given the foregoing, if Mat Crichton had shot his father in the forehead as Sandy approached, it might have been regarded as a public service. The fact that the shot is fired after Sandy turned is directly related to not only the relationship, but also to the conditions existing in the shop that day (lighting in particular) combined with Mat's disabilities (in particular vision and processing speed) resulting from his frontal lobe injury.

MAT CRICHTON

It is expected that Mat Crichton would testify that after his father chased him with the tractor, he exited the bobcat and ran /walked/limped to his shop. He decided that he was not going to run away but for once in his life would take steps to defend himself if his father pursued his assault. He went to the shop and began to load his .22. His father surprised him by appearing in the doorway. He hadn't heard him approach. He must have come on foot, which was very unusual because he didn't walk anywhere. He always took the tractor or a quad.

Mat warned Sandy that he had a gun. Sandy replied "Bull-shit" or something like that and continued into the shop towards Mat. Mat raised the gun to fire a warning shot, but the gun would not discharge. As his father approached he lowered the gun, realizing the safety was on, and tried to release it. He did so, immediately lifted the gun and fired. He hadn't seen his father turn or retreat. Following the shot he approached and looked at his father and realized that he must have turned. He thought or maybe hoped that his father had died of a heart attack.

DR. JACK KEEGAN

An expert witness, neuropsychologist and clinical psychologist. In 2005 he examined Matthew Crichton following the motor vehicle accident and prepared a report which detailed many of Mat's deficits resulting from the injury to his left temporal lobe. You have been provided with his 2005 report. In 2011 Dr. Keegan was retained by the defence to essentially update his 2005 report and give a current picture of Mat's various deficits. He was also asked to examine in particular Mat's "processing speed," that is, how Mat's brain processes information in order that he may make choices and act upon that information. Dr. Keegan administered a battery of standard tests. As a result of that objective testing, Dr. Keegan found that on a measure of simple reaction time sensitive to arousal, attention, and processing speed impairments, performance was severely impaired at almost half normal levels. He was administered a choice reaction time test twice, and in each instance performance was extremely impaired, with performance roughly four times worse than the norm (i.e., taking four times longer to make and act upon very simple tasks—"press the button if you see a triangle").

Following testing Dr. Keegan was supplied with a hypothetical (similar to Mat Crichton's expected testimony, above) as well as relevant photographs and the findings of the ophthalmologist, Dr. Daniel Senekal (see below). Dr. Keegan was asked to comment as to how Mat Crichton's disabilities would affect his perceptions at the time of the shooting, and in particular to address the fact that the shot was fired evidently after Sandy Crichton had turned and that normally one might comprehend that the threat had dissipated. It is expected that Dr. Keegan would say:

> Based upon my understanding of Mr. Crichton's visual limitations, in combination with clear evidence of slowed information processing speed, and put together with the likely further diminished perceptual abilities based upon externally induced hyperarousal, it is, in my view, improbable that Mr. Crichton was able to either perceive or effectively react to the change of risk assumed to be associated with the father's retreat. I believe it is not likely that Mr. Crichton perceived the change in circumstances occasioned by his father's retreat.
>
> There are two aspects to this; one is the basic sensory aspect. There is evidence to suggest fundamental limitations in what Mr. Crichton was *physically able to see* (see below); and, secondly, there is the *perceptual* aspect. That is how Mr. Crichton takes whatever his visual system was able to apprehend and subsequently translates that into actionable information. Perception involves the process of interpretation of the sensory experience. Slow reaction time and slow information processing means that this process would, in all likelihood, be seriously slowed especially in the circumstances in question. Slow information processing speed also results in problems with multitasking, which have been observed by others in his immediate environment. Problems with multitasking further create even greater interference with the perceptual act, and it is, in fact, likely that under the

circumstances as I understand them, he would pull the trigger or take action prior to having full or even any realization of the change of circumstances (i.e., his father turning or retreating).

My assessment of Mr. Crichton indicates to me that as the complexity of task requirements increases, his reaction time becomes even more markedly slower. Given all that I am aware of with regard to Mr. Crichton, it is my view that it is likely he did not recognize the change in circumstances arising from his father's retreat at the time that he pulled the trigger. His long history of abuse at the hands of his father would also be seen as affecting his perception in this regard, because experience with his father was not such that his father ever retreated. His perception of his father's actions would be coloured by that history. Essentially, his expectancies regarding his father's likely aggression become a potent factor in the interpretation or perception of vague sensory input.

In summary, it is my view that there are both sensory and perceptual elements that would significantly impact on Mr. Crichton's understanding of what was occurring at the time he shot his father. Perceptual aspects are affected by significant cognitive limitations arising from brain damage and historical expectancies.

MIKE REEVES: is expected to say that he is a professional photographer and that in the summer of 2011 he was retained by the defence to take photographs inside the shop where the shot was fired. The photographs were to depict as closely as possible the lighting conditions and visibility within the shop. September 3, 2010, was a bright sunny day and on a similar day in September 2011 Mr. Reeves attended the shop and took several photographs. His cameras were placed toward the rear of the shop near the location of the gun safe. The settings on the cameras were adjusted to duplicate the vision of the normal human eye. Photographs were taken of a subject (height 5'10", weight 220 pounds) as that person entered the shop, proceeded 3–4 paces and then turned and exited. Those photos are attached, and Mr. Reeves would testify that not only were they taken in accord with his training and technical recommendations for replicating what the human eye sees, they do in fact replicate what he was able to see that day.

Upon review of the photographs you will note that even for the uninvolved (rather than panic-stricken) ordinary eye, it is very difficult to discern whether the silhouette is facing or backing.

DR. DANIEL SENEKAL: is expected to say that he is both a medical doctor and an ophthalmologist, duly trained and qualified. In 2011 Dr. Senekal was retained by the defence to better explore the problems with Mat's vision which were documented by various physicians (including Dr. Keegan) following the motor vehicle accident in 2004. Dr. Senekal conducted testing which revealed that Mat's field of vision is severely restricted as illustrated by the attached chart. In addition, when Dr. Senekal was advised of the lighting conditions which existed in the shop the day of the shooting, he had Mat attend the University of Alberta for "darkness adaptation testing" in order to determine how Mat's eyes react to change in lighting, particularly darkening conditions. The result of that testing was that Mat's eyes showed "no rod contribution" to his vision. The significance of that deficit is explained by Dr. Senekal: Dark adaptation can therefore not occur normally, and only the Cones will contribute to the limited amount of dark adaptation. Rods are the photoreceptors responsible for: 1. Our ability to function and see in conditions of low lighting; 2. Our ability to detect motion; and 3. Peripheral vision. All three of these visual tasks are significantly reduced or impaired with a Rod Dystrophy.

In other words, Mat's eyes adapt to darkened conditions (going from bright sunny day to dim lighting of shop) much less than the normal eye, and his ability to see his father would not be as depicted in the photos. It would be much more limited. In addition, his ability to perceive movement (i.e., his father turning) would be limited by deficits in his rods, his peripheral vision.

THE LAW
R v. Kandola [1993] BCJ No 1035 (BCCA) is both analogous and authoritative. In that case the Accused was threatened in his home by a group of men standing outside. The Accused fired

what was intended to be a warning shot from his upper window. That shot killed one of the persons outside and the Accused was charged with second-degree murder. At trial he was convicted. The appeal was allowed and an acquittal directed, the Court noting variously as follows:

Dealing with the requirements of s. 34(1), the trial judge found:

(a) The appellant was unlawfully assaulted.

(b) The appellant did not provoke the assault upon himself.

(c) The appellant was justified in repelling force by force.

(d) He had a reasonable doubt whether the appellant intended to cause death or grievous bodily harm.

(e) The force used by the appellant—firing a warning shot without aiming it at his assailant—was no more than was necessary to enable him to defend himself.

These findings lead inescapably to the legal conclusion that the act of shooting to warn was justified and therefore not an unlawful act, with the result the death of Santokh Singh Sandhu was not a culpable homicide; *Regina v. Baker* (1988), 45 C.C.C. (3d) 368.

The second reason which leads me to conclude the trial judge erred in his approach to s. 34(1) is the fact the law has long recognized the need for a tolerant approach to the objective measurement of proportionate force in genuine self-defence cases. In *Brown v. United States* (1921), 256 U.S. 335, at p. 343, Holmes, J., noted:

• Detached reflection cannot be demanded in the presence of an uplifted knife.

A similar expression of opinion was voiced by Lord Morris in *Palmer v. The Queen* (1971), 55 Cr. App. R. 223, at p. 242 of the report:

• If there has been attack so that defence is reasonably necessary, it will be recognized that a person defending himself cannot weigh to a nicety the exact measure of his necessary defensive action.

The same principle has been adopted and applied by Canadian courts: see, for example; *Rex v. Ogal* (1928), 50 C.C.C. 71 (Alta. S.C. App. Div.), at pp. 73–4, *Regina v. Preston* (1953), 106 C.C.C. 135 (B.C.C.A.), at p. 140, *Regina v. Antley,* [1964] 2 C.C.C. 142 (Ont. C.A.), at p. 147, and *Regina v. Baxter* (1975), 27 C.C.C. (2d) 96 (Ont. C.A.), at p. 111.

It would be inconsistent with this principle to expect a person who is under an attack of sufficient magnitude to warrant resort to potentially deadly force, even though no deadly intent is present, to stop and reflect upon the risk of deadly consequences which might result from taking such defensive action.

I suggest that the same justification is applicable to the case under consideration, and as a result I further respectfully suggest that the intention of the Accused is well accounted for, both in fact and in law. A warning shot was entirely justifiable. In fact if he shot to kill it would very arguably be justifiable. The result should be, at this stage, the realization that the Crown truly has a problematic case, and both sides should be motivated to resolve uncertainties which always attend a trial, by a sensible plea. That plea would be to criminal negligence causing death but without reliance upon the aggravating feature of the firearm. This will escape the mandatory minimum provisions and ought to result in a suspended sentence (or similar disposition) given all of the very unique features of this case.

Yours Truly,
David R. Cunningham DRC/DMT

         ❦

Dave and the Crown prosecutors reached an agreement that Mat would plead guilty to manslaughter. The Crown earned our respect by making the most reasonable offer they could. Now Mat's final hearing lay ahead.

CHAPTER 28

WHEN IT WAS decided Mat would plead guilty to manslaughter, the date for sentencing was moved to December 9, 2011. Crown prosecutor Jasmine Sihra reached an agreement with Dave Cunningham on what they would ask the judge to rule. Both the prosecution and the defence were hoping Judge Golden could overlook the fact that a firearm was used, so as not to trigger the mandatory minimum sentence. Before the courtroom opened, Dave called Mat, Jenny, and me into a small meeting room and explained what would likely happen, so we wouldn't be surprised by anything.

There was no need for a crowd of supporters at the sentencing hearing, since there was nothing more anyone could do to help Mat's case. Jenny and her dad sat close together near the front of the courtroom. Sherry Lofstrom and I sat together toward the back of the room, with my wheelchair sticking out in the aisle. The only other member of our team who was there was Roy Carter, who had walked over from his office nearby to hear the sentence. Mat, slim and clean shaven, wearing his good Wrangler jeans, new boots, belt, and the western style dress shirt he'd worn at his wedding, sat at the table beside Dave Cunningham.

For Mat's plea of "guilty to the charge of manslaughter" to be accepted, Judge Golden had to be presented with an Agreed Statement of Facts, the circumstances as agreed to by both the Crown and the defence. The Crown prosecutor read the statement aloud in the courtroom. Dave had explained the procedure to us, saying that it would be up to the judge to decide on the sentence after he heard the agreed-upon statement of facts.

"These are the agreed statement of facts," the prosecutor began. "On September 3, 2010, at 11:56 hours Matthew Gordon

Crichton, hereafter referred to as the accused, called 911 and said that he had just shot his seventy-three-year-old father. The accused further stated that he had put up with his father for twenty-seven years and had had enough. The accused provided the location of the incident, the family farm, which was near Grovedale, Alberta, and guided police there.

"At the location given, police found Alexander Crichton, the victim, lying on his stomach just outside the doorway of the accused's workshop. The victim was assessed and it was determined that he was deceased.

"The accused was very co-operative with the police and provided two audio/videotaped cautioned statements. He provided a full confession to shooting his father. The accused provided an outline of the family's troubled history and the details of the events which led to him shooting his father.

"The accused and the victim had a very unstable relationship since the accused was a child. The victim had a bad temper and had been physically and verbally abusive towards his family and others. The accused was a passenger in a motor vehicle accident in 2004, as a result of which he was in a coma for about a month and suffered brain damage. The accused's reaction to the victim's actions on September 3, 2010, was coloured by his past experiences with the victim, as well as sensory and perceptual deficits.

"The accused lived on the same farm property as his parents, along with his new wife, whom he had married on August 22, 2010. On September 2, the accused and his wife, Jennifer, returned from their honeymoon in British Columbia. Jennifer was, at the time of the offence, approximately three months pregnant with the couple's first child.

"On September 3, at around midday the accused began to move loads of gravel with the bobcat to fix some potholes on one of the farm roads on their property. His father came out and for some reason, upset over what the accused was doing, began yelling at him. The victim tried to enter the cab of the bobcat. The accused manoeuvred the bobcat, pushing the victim away. The victim was yelling and swearing at the accused to come off the bobcat, but the accused thought that if he did the victim would kick his ass.

"The victim went and got a nearby tractor. The accused saw the victim coming quickly down the road towards him. The accused then started driving away on the bobcat. The tractor was bigger and faster than the bobcat, so the accused drove behind a large piece of farm equipment to hide. The accused then got out of the bobcat and started running away on foot. His father got off the tractor and started after the accused; however, the accused was faster and outdistanced him.

"The accused ran to some nearby hay bales, then made his way into his shop. The accused heard some noise with the tractor outside and thought his father may have been moving the gravel pile the accused had just put on the road.

"Based on the history of abuse by his father towards himself and others and his father's anger outside, the accused was apprehensive that the situation with his father might escalate. The accused went to one side of the shop to get the safe combination from under a cabinet and then went to the other side of the shop to open his gun safe. The accused obtained the combination for the safe, which he wrote on his hand. The accused then proceeded to open the safe within which were a 30-30 rifle and a .22-calibre handgun.

"The accused removed the handgun and began to load the clip. He had three shells in the clip when his father appeared at the door of the shop and began to yell at him. The victim was shouting about what the accused had been doing with the gravel outside and came towards the accused. The accused warned, I'm getting a gun. The victim said something to the effect of, bullshit. The accused raised the gun and pulled the trigger twice, but with no result. Realizing the safety had been on, the accused released it and fired. The victim had turned away from the accused. The shot fired a distance of approximately fifty feet when the accused was inside the shop and the victim was in the doorway. It struck the victim in the back of the neck, killing him.

"Following the shot, the accused approached and looked at his father. The accused could not see where the victim had been hit. The victim was just lying there and was not moving or saying anything. The accused then called 911 as detailed in the foregoing."

"And those are the facts that are acknowledged?" the court asked.

"Yes, sir, they are," replied Mr. Cunningham.

"Very well, then, the guilty plea is accepted."

Judge Golden excused himself, saying that he would be back shortly with Mat's sentence. I could see Dave and Mat talking to each other. Jenny, Denis, Sherry, Roy, and I sat in silence. There was nothing to say. After a short while, Judge Golden came back into the courtroom, adjusted his papers on the desk in front of him, and then explained the term he was sentencing Matti to, and began his address.

He thanked the counsel on both sides for their hard work in coming to an agreement on what they felt Mat's sentence should be. "This was a tragic situation," he said, "that had befallen a family who had been subjected to one tragic event after another."

Sentences for manslaughter ranged from a suspended sentence to life imprisonment, Judge Golden explained, but where a firearm had been involved in the offence, the court was required to impose a minimum sentence of forty-eight months or four years.

The judge noted that Mat had no history of conduct that would suggest he was a threat to the community or to others. "In fact," Judge Golden went on, "the letters from the community strongly suggested otherwise. From the outset, Mat had co-operated with the police. Immediately after the incident he had called 911. He had acknowledged what he had done right from the outset.

"There had been a long history of violence perpetrated on Matthew Crichton at the hands of his father, Alex Crichton," the judge continued. "That abuse appears random and unprovoked. The impression left with the court is that Alex Crichton was a time bomb waiting to explode. No one knew when that would occur or why it would occur. When his temper raged he was out of control, both with people and with animals. Alex Crichton's abuse of Matthew had continued after Matthew's injuries were sustained in 2004, and may have even escalated after that period of time."

Judge Golden said that the court had never seen so many letters from neighbours, relatives, professionals, or other members of the community. That all those letters were written for the purpose of supporting Mat's release showed Mat was not a danger. He also noted that the letters had been written by simple acquaintances as well as people who had an intimate knowledge of Mat. For acquaintances to have taken the time to generate such letters, he said, was an indication of the respect the community had for Mat. The judge noted as well that continuing the farm operation would be difficult without Mat's help.

When Judge Golden was finished speaking, he gathered his papers and left. The sheriff stood patiently beside Mat as he hugged us one by one. Jenny, Sherry, Denis, and I were all crying openly. After the hugs, Mat took off his prized western belt, with the trophy buckle his friend had given him for good luck after his accident, and handed it to Jenny, saying he wouldn't be needing it for a while.

My heart broke to see my son being led away to prison. But I was comforted by the knowledge that, barring any incident, he would be able to do his time as sentenced and then get back home.

That evening, Roy Carter sent an e-mail to a large group of friends and supporters.

> Mat was sentenced to 4 years today on a guilty plea of Manslaughter. The judge said that was the minimum sentence he could impose given changes to the Criminal Code that require a 4-year minimum if a firearm is used in a death. He referred to similar cases prior to the new legislation where one accused even received a suspended sentence. Clearly the judge wanted to give a lesser sentence, as he said the legislation was never meant to apply to such a situation. However, he was bound by the law.
>
> Defence and Crown had asked for 30 months and to have the judge "ignore" that a firearm was used, but Judge Golden said he could not do that. Too bad the government took away the discretion of the judges, as it really hurt Mat here.

So then the judge went to work to try and mitigate
the minimum sentence. He gave Mat a credit of one
for one for each day of house arrest on the farm, so
he gets 11 months credit here for house arrest. Plus, he
received a two for one credit for his time in Peace River.
In all, he gets a 15-month credit. So effectively he has
a 33-month sentence to serve starting today. The judge
is suggesting the Grande Cache Correctional Centre
in due course.

For the judge, the community support was huge.
He said the Court had never seen this type of support,
and he talked of the hundreds of letters of support in
regards to the bail hearing.

When the judge asked Mat if he had anything to
say, Mat said, "I'm sorry to have caused so much trouble. I never meant to kill my dad. I just wanted to fire a
warning shot. I never meant to hurt anyone."

CHAPTER 29

DAVE CUNNINGHAM HAD told me before Mat's sentencing hearing that when Mat got to prison, he shouldn't ask any of the inmates what they were in for. The inmates had their own laws, he said, and Mat should just quietly mind his own business. I assumed Dave had meant, also, that Mat shouldn't tell the other inmates what he was in for.

When I warned Mat about that, he asked me, "What am I supposed to do if someone asks me why I'm in prison?"

"I have no idea," I said. "But you'll have to think of something."

Mat was sent first to the Peace River Correctional Institute, where he'd been initially, then to the Edmonton Remand Centre. He was shipped to the Grande Cache Correctional Centre a few days before Christmas.

Even though Dave had told me that Grande Cache was the safest prison for Mat to be in, the dark shadow cast by fear never went away. Every time the phone rang, my stomach churned until I found out who the caller was and what the call was about. When the phone didn't ring, I imagined that something horrible had happened to prevent Mat from calling me. The prisoners had been locked down, or he'd been injured. My imagination ran wild.

Shortly after he arrived at Grande Cache, Mat said to me on the phone, "I know you told me not to tell anyone what I'm in here for, but I had to."

My skin prickled.

"When I got to the prison, the guards put me in a cell," he continued. "As soon as they left, this huge prisoner came into my cell. He told me to come with him. I had no choice."

Christ, I thought, *now what?*

"I followed him. There were about ten inmates waiting for me. Staring at me. The main guy said, 'What are you in for?' I had no choice. I had to tell them."

"What did you tell them?"

"Everything."

"What did they say?"

"The head guy said, 'You better not be lying. I'm gonna get my buddy on the outside to check it out. If you're lying, you'll be sorry!'"

Thank God he hadn't listened to me. Every minute at home was filled with apprehension, knowing there wasn't a thing I could do to help Mat. Thankfully, that soon began to change. Dave Cunningham sent me an e-mail saying there was something I should see. The Crown prosecutor had taken the unprecedented step of writing a note she included with Mat's prison intake papers.

> Re: Matthew Crichton. The Court recommended that the accused be permitted to serve his sentence at the Grande Cache facility as it is closer to home. The Crown very strongly supports this recommendation as the accused would benefit greatly from family support. The accused has cognitive and physical challenges due to a 2004 brain injury. The victim of the manslaughter charge to which the accused pled guilty was the accused's tyrannical father who had been verbally and physically abusive for years to the accused and others, including his wheelchair-bound mother. Dozens of reference letters produced at the sentencing attest that the accused is a non-violent person. Given the foregoing, it would be greatly appreciated if penitentiary staff "look out" for this accused.

To my profound gratitude and relief, connections with a number of prison guards began to emerge via friends and acquaintances. Every conversation I had and every connection that was made on Mat's behalf served to humanize the prison staff for me. Their kindness and caring helped to erase the vision I had from movies and television of prison guards as cruel, hard people. The guards I spoke with told me, emphatically, that Mat could not know they were looking out for him. He would be in danger if other prisoners felt he was being favoured in any way. So it wasn't until he came home that Mat learned he had had friends and guardian angels all around him.

Not long after Mat arrived at Grande Cache, I spoke on the phone with a guard who worked there. "I shouldn't really be talking to you," he said, "but I met Mat a few years ago, and I liked him. I'm very sorry to see him in this situation. I can't do anything directly to help him, but maybe I can help you understand how the system works."

I expressed my gratitude, asking him to tell me anything he could to enlighten me.

He said, "My greatest worry is that Mat will be mistaken for a sex offender, which would instantly brand him, and set him up for abuse and harassment. The fact that he walks with a limp and speaks slowly singles him out and makes him noticeable. But it would go badly for Mat if any of the other prisoners think I'm a friend to him."

"I understand," I said.

"When Mat first arrived," he told me, "I used an excuse to get him into a room, with another prison staff person present, to try to give him a heads-up. I think I might have been a bit harsh with him, but I wanted him to have no doubt as to the fact that we cannot be friends in the prison."

"I heard he shouldn't be telling anyone why he's in there," I said.

"Not so," said the guard. "The first thing the other inmates want to know is what a newcomer is in for. If the person is evasive, it could be seen as them trying to hide the fact that they are a sex offender, the lowest denominator in the system. Sex offenders, especially pedophiles, do not want to tell their story. Mat should be careful not to become friends with one. He should just stay low profile, possibly watch to see which prisoners are respected and associate with them. There are guys who are respected by both sides, usually men who are in for long sentences and just want to get their time over with. There are a lot of decent guys who have just done stupid things. But there are also a lot of really bad guys."

I listened to the guard's advice closely, taking notes as he spoke.

"Mat should tell someone if he is getting targeted or bullied," he concluded. "The way to do so is with a *kite*, which means writing the offence down and slipping it to a guard without being seen to do so. Then no one knows who told. There are bad guys on staff, too. If they are ignorant, or tell Mat to do something, he should just listen and not argue. The same if inmates want to boss him around, unless it gets out of hand."

I was still cautious about what I said on the phone, assuming my calls with Mat could be monitored at any time. I waited until Jenny, Percy, and I went to see him in Grande Cache to tell him about the kites.

In order for Mat to be able to call us on the phone, purchase a small TV, or buy little extras from the canteen, Jenny and I sent cheques to the finance department at the prison. They deposited the money to Mat's account, and he could then use it as a credit.

Often when Mat called, he'd talk about the disturbing behaviour some of the inmates displayed. Sometimes that was frightening for him. Other times it made him feel sorry for the individual. One fellow he mentioned numerous times frightened Mat, because Mat felt like the guy was watching him. The inmate was obviously a king pin, tattooed and muscular, from Mat's description. Mat said the man could lift all the weights in the gym at once.

As Mat and I were talking on the phone one evening, I heard someone make a comment in the background. Mat said to me under his breath, "That's him, the guy I was telling you about."

I heard Mat say, "It's my mom I'm talking to."

Tattooed Guy, in the background, said, "Tell her 'hi' from me."

"Here. Do you want to talk to her?" Mat asked him.

I heard the phone rustle as Mat passed it to Tattooed Guy. *Jesus, Mat,* I thought. *What the heck am I going to talk to a big, scary prisoner about?*

Tattooed Guy said, "Hi, Mrs. Crichton." From his manner he could easily have been an insurance salesman or a banker.

"Hello," I said. "How are you?"

"I'm fine," he said. The blood left my body when I heard his next statement. "Mrs. Crichton, I just want you to know that we're looking out for your boy in here."

I'd heard through various sources that an employee at the prison had called in a favour from one of the high-ranking prisoners, asking that he look out for Mat. I'd thought the story was too good to be true, but I realized with a shock that I'd been wrong. Mat's instinct that Tattooed Guy was watching him had been correct all along.

CHAPTER 30

THE PRISON STAFF in Grande Cache were always helpful and considerate when Jenny and I visited Mat, even giving Percy little treats when he was with us. From Mat's parole officer, Sue McClure, I learned that Mat was entitled to a hearing in July to determine if he'd be released on day parole. Sue would be recommending that he receive it, she told me.

Through my research on the internet, I discovered that I would be entitled to stand up for Mat at the hearing as an "Offender's Assistant." I could also present Jenny's thoughts to the parole board. Jenny and I weren't sure whether we should have a lawyer represent Mat at the hearing or do it ourselves. Dave Cunningham had retired shortly after Mat's sentencing. It would be complicated to use a lawyer who didn't know Mat, and, by that time, the dollars were tight. Jenny was paid for a year of maternity leave, and thankfully Mat had a small monthly annuity from his accident that had been tiding them over financially. The money we got for selling the cows had paid the lawyer's fees. Laurie had stayed to help out on the farm in Mat's absence, and the income from our small flock of ewes paid her a wage. I was still receiving my workers' compensation pension. We were downsized, but getting by. I knew I could do this job. I knew the case inside out, and I knew Mat.

Sue McClure gave me advice on what the parole board would be looking for.

Mat alarmed me during a phone call by telling me what he had prepared himself to read to the parole board. Thank goodness he'd decided to run it by me. He started out by saying, "I'm sorry for taking the law into my own hands with vigilante justice." When I asked him where he got the idea to say something like that, he told me he'd seen it on a TV show and thought it sounded good. He was shaken when I explained how the words made it sound as if he had set out to shoot his father on purpose.

As Mat's parole officer, Sue would be spending some time with him before the hearing, preparing him for it. She told me he'd be allowed to read a written statement, and she indicated that the best approach for him would be to keep it short and simple. She also warned me that the board would question Mat extensively, and that the questioning could be quite intense. The closer we got to the hearing, the more I second-guessed myself. *What am I thinking?* I agonized. What gave me the idea I could represent Mat before a parole board? I had no idea what I was doing. But I knew Mat better than anyone else on earth, and I'd do my utmost to represent him well. There was no turning back now.

On the day of the hearing Jenny's mom kept Percy for her, and we left home at 5:30 a.m. to arrive at the correctional centre by 7:00. We went through the usual routine of getting our personal items examined, then being checked by a drug sniffer dog and going through a scanner. By now, we were old hands at a process that at one time had made us uncomfortable and nervous.

We were directed to the meeting room where we always went for visits with Mat. Before long, a parole officer we didn't know came in and spoke with us, outlining what would take place at the hearing. As she leafed through Matti's file, she stopped to read a particular page. "I've never seen this happen before," she said to us. "Do you realize the Crown prosecutor sent a note with Mat's file asking us to watch out for him?"

We told her we did know that. We'd heard it from every person who'd read Mat's file. Every one of them said they'd never seen it happen before.

The officer escorted Jenny and me through the prison to the infirmary, where we were to wait until being called into the meeting room. Sue McClure joined us there and went over the hearing procedure with us again. She read my short presentation and said it looked fine. She'd outlined to Mat what the board's questions for him would be as well. I was calm and collected by this time. I knew we were all going to do the best we could, and I hoped it would be good enough.

We were called into the meeting room, and as usual it was awkward getting situated because of my wheelchair. A few chairs had to be moved for me to get to my spot at the conference table. The air conditioning was down, Sue had warned us, and the entire prison was stiflingly hot. A large fan on a stand blew full force directly behind where Jenny and I were seated. My voice doesn't project well, and I hoped the board would be able to hear me above the roaring of the fan.

Three men sat on the opposite side of the conference table: the two parole review officers and a scribe who would take notes. On our side of the table, Mat was seated furthest from the door. I was reminded of the old days when I'd been an apprentice jockey, scared to death as I faced three racing stewards across a table.

I could see numerous handwritten notes on the pages of the thick binder each of the parole review officers had in front of him. It was obvious they had reviewed Mat's case thoroughly in preparation. The scribe introduced everyone, and each of the review officers took a turn relaying what he knew of the case. The board asked Sue McClure to give her recommendation. After she had endorsed her written opinion that Mat should be released on parole, the review officers turned to Mat. Sue had prepared him to be asked questions related to his future plans and whether he felt remorse for killing his father. The review officers surprised us all by saying to him instead, "Tell us what happened that day."

Before they asked him to tell them the story, Mat had never related what happened on the day of the shooting to anyone but the police, Dave Cunningham, Roy Carter, Jenny, and me. Because of the way the cops had manipulated what Mat said when they interrogated him, I was nervous about the request. I thought maybe this was going to be more of the same. But as Mat told his story for the first time since before his sentencing a year and a half earlier, the intensity of what he had experienced was obvious. The room was silent as we listened to him.

When Mat was done talking, the review officers indicated I should begin my presentation. I took a sip of water and began. As Sue had advised me, I talked about Mat's character and his work ethic.

NO WAY TO RUN   207

"I'm a lot closer to Mat than most mothers would be to their adult son, because of his brain injury," I told the board. "When his injury happened in 2004, I was told he might always be a vegetable, or severely disabled, and that I should get power of attorney over his affairs. I didn't, because I was determined to do everything in my power to help Mat become a productive, independent man once again. I spent a number of years working with him toward that goal, starting from square one.

"Mat never once complained, though his body and his brain were both severely damaged. He just dug deeper and tried harder. It was that attitude that brought him to the attention of the entire community and earned him their respect. It doesn't matter where I go, someone will come up to me and ask how he's doing, expressing concern and support for him."

Dave Cunningham had also given me some advice on how to prepare for the hearing, I told the panel. That advice was, "Emphasis should be placed on Judge Golden's finding that he didn't believe Mat was a danger to the community, the Crown's concurrence in the report they provided, and the fact that Mat's behaviour at the correctional centre here has not contradicted either of those predictions."

I'd brought copies of some relevant documents to the hearing, I informed the parole board, including seven of the 260 letters of support Mat had received, the Agreed Statement of Facts, the psychologist's report, Dr. Senekal's report, the Transcript of Sentencing, and the Victim's Statement I had prepared for the judge.

"Mat is one of the most diligent, honest, hard-working people I know," I concluded, "and as one of the support letters written for Mat points out, he is guileless. In my opinion, the best thing that could happen for all involved would be for Mat to come home to his wife and son and go to work on the farm."

When I finished reading, one of the parole review officers asked me if I felt any differently toward Mat after Sandy's death. "No, I don't," I replied. "None of our family does. It was a terrible thing to happen, but we do not blame Mat for it."

Since I was the person officially speaking on Mat's behalf, I read Jenny's statement next. "When I first met Mat in 2009," she had written, "I could tell right away what kind of man he is.

For starters, I cannot express enough how hard-working he is. There's never a moment he'll sit and rest unless it's mealtime, because there's always work to be done on the farm.

"I've often teased him about how many projects he has on the go at one time, aside from the regular farm maintenance, but anyone who knows Mat will say that's normal. He's always busy thinking of new eco-friendly ways to improve our way of living around the place, and somehow finds time to fit them into his schedule, because that's his passion. Even while he's been at Grande Cache prison, he tells me every day about new ideas of what he wants to do. I just shake my head and laugh, because he will do it somehow...

"Mat is an amazingly loyal and loving man as well. He and his mother share a bond I've rarely seen with adult children and their parents. They've been through so much together that they're connected on many levels. He'll do anything for his mother, and she for him. Mat is also a father, and a naturally amazing one at that. Ever since the idea of our son, he's loved him unconditionally. Even when we were told the worst about the future our son may have, that love never changed...

"I could go on for pages about Mat and who he is as a person, but the truth is, none of my words will truly show you what kind of person he is. When he is truly Mat, he is on the farm doing what he loves every day, and I love him for that."

The parole review officers asked us to leave the room, and we waited anxiously for twenty minutes until we were called back. To our great joy and relief, they announced that they were granting Mat day parole, and also full parole as soon as he was eligible.

Mat's earliest possible release date wasn't for another four months, so arrangements were made for him to spend that time at a halfway house in Edmonton. During the time he was there, the thoroughbreds were racing at Edmonton's Northlands Park. Donald Gilkyson, a racehorse trainer and family friend, got Mat a groom's licence and found him a job grooming racehorses for Dino Helfenstein, another family friend. I was very pleased Mat would be among friends at the racetrack. I knew they'd look out for him. The thoroughbreds raced at Northlands until late October, so Mat only had a few days to fill after they left before he could come home.

Mat returned home on full parole on November 6, 2012. The first thing we did was have Ged Willis from the Beaverlodge Auction Mart buy twenty-four cows for us, and his son delivered them to the farm. Priority number two for Mat was hooking up our little utility trailer and heading to a local Hutterite colony to buy a bred sow. When I saw him return with her, I headed out on my power chair to have a look.

He backed up to the barn door, dropped the endgate on the trailer and called out, "Come on, Princess, this is your new home."

I angled around so I could see into the trailer. Princess was lurking in the back corner, straw up to her low-hanging belly, her little piggy eyes blinking at the glare bombarding her from the open trailer door. She'd never been outside of the huge pig barn where she was born and raised.

Princess was not going to walk out into the shockingly cold, glaringly bright, snow-covered world of the great outdoors. Rather than force her, Mat left the trailer parked overnight with the door open. I watched from the house window the next morning as Princess timidly shambled on wobbly legs, shivering, off the trailer and into the barn. It took her nearly a month to adjust, but by the time her piglets were born, she was no longer just a princess. She was queen of the barnyard.

CHAPTER 31

AFTER A RELATIVELY mild winter, a blizzard is raging outside, and it's twenty below. I'm sitting at the kitchen table in my cozy house, looking out at the cows hunched up with their tails turned toward the blowing snow. In a nearby corral, the ewes are huddled together in a snowy lump. Next to them, Mat's pigs are buried in the straw. On the wall in front of me hangs a photo taken February 15, 2013, the day the community celebration for Mat and Jenny's wedding was finally held.

After all the drama we'd been through, Mat and Jenny had questioned whether they should go ahead with the party. But Jenny's grandparents from the Okanagan were adamant that Jenny have a celebration, and that they be there. Mat's seventh-grade teacher, Jim Biggs, who had corresponded with Mat while he was in prison, agreed to be the master of ceremonies. When I approached Laurie Bowen, the caterer for the community club, she said that if we paid for the food she would get a volunteer crew together to prepare it. Another friend, Doreen Bezovie, took charge of decorating the hall with things she had saved from her own kids' weddings.

It's hard to describe the gratitude I felt as I looked at the familiar faces that filled the hall that evening. Whether through moral support, a kind word, or simply being present, each person there had given a piece of themselves to make our family better and stronger. It was the grandest celebration I could imagine.

When I was a young jockey, I'd vowed to live as fast and as hard as I could. At times now, I feel like an old battery that's been used too long and left out in the cold. Once I'm warmed up and pampered a bit, though, there's still enough juice in me to crank over and get the job done. When I'm feeling drained, I think of all the amazing people I know. Many of them have fought tremendous battles against overwhelming odds and managed to keep going. They give me strength and energy. And I owe a debt to the hundreds of people who have had the courage to stand up for me and my family. Telling our story is my way of bearing witness.

Peaceful is how I would describe the aura of our farm now. That in itself sometimes alarms me. I feel as if I'm missing something, not being alert enough. Not watching my back. But those times are getting fewer.

It's never dull at the farm. People are constantly coming and going. For two years we hosted the local 4H lamb club, keeping the lambs here and having the kids come over for meetings and to work with their lambs regularly. There's no longer a 4H club, but the South Wapiti Readers book club is headquartered here, with meetings every two weeks.

Mat and Jenny pick up the slack by doing chores that I can't do. They get my groceries, go to the library, and do the odd bit of running around for me when there is too much snow for me to manoeuvre in Grande Prairie on my wheelchair. They're also on call to come and pull me out when I get my power chair stuck in the snow or mud, which happens all too often. Mat and Marie McCullough, a good friend who used to train horses with me and is now our local municipal district grader operator, keep the roads cleared so I can walk my dogs every day. Rain, snow, or shine, I bundle up, and get outside for a walk. It grounds me.

Our old cat Wilbur, his glossy orange coat faded to a dull yellow, died two winters ago. He slipped quietly off as he lay on the floor in my bathroom, in the spot where he never failed to thank me with a purr as I brushed him every morning. Once he was gone, I made it clear to everyone that I would not have another cat in the house. Too much of a nuisance with the litter box and cat hair, I said. We needed barn cats, though, so I sent Jenny to the SPCA to pick up a couple. She came home with two cats in a little portable kennel: a black neutered male that bolted as soon as she opened the gate and a spayed calico named Maisie, who instantly went over to Percy and made friends.

If cats could speak, Maisie would have been shouting at Jenny, "Wait a minute! The pound got it all wrong. I am *not* a barn cat! Never was. Never will be!" She now lives in my house, and I'm very fond of her, despite the cat hair and litter box. I often wonder where she originated, and if anyone misses her. The black cat disappeared two days after his arrival. We have no idea if he left home, or if an owl or a coyote got him. Jenny picked up two more neutered cats from the SPCA. One promptly disappeared, but the other one is still here. He's buddied up with Marty, the only old barn cat we have left.

Hobo, the old Great Pyrenees dog, had to be put down. He was at least thirteen, and although we treated him on a daily basis with glucosamine and aspirin, he was suffering badly. Even so, he insisted on coming for walks with me every day. If I tied him up and left him behind, he'd whine his anguish as he gazed at the rest of the pack following along behind my wheelchair. It broke my heart to make the decision to end his life, but I knew his time on earth was up.

The farm is surrounded by wilderness. Our closest neighbours are cougars, black bears, grizzly bears, wolves, coyotes, and lynx. We depend on our livestock guardian dogs to keep them out of the yard area. Not that our guardian dogs could handle large predators in a battle, but they do make it annoying and inconvenient for anything trying to sneak around. They also keep ungulates like deer, elk, and moose from destroying the haystacks.

Three years ago, with our guardian dog getting old, we knew we had to get a replacement for him. We purchased a Great Pyrenees puppy and named him Phil. I'm sure he weighs well over 120 pounds now. We liked Phil so much that we bought a full brother, two years younger, and named him Charlie. He's nearly full-grown now and works all night alongside Phil, guarding the livestock.

I still have my border collies Glen and Zeke. They, along with Maisie, sleep in the house with me. Zeke sticks close to my wheelchair these days. He's stone deaf, getting senile, and is terribly insecure. His tumble from unquestioned ruler of the farmyard, willing to do anything I asked of him, to a doddering old creature, makes my heart ache. But he still thinks he's top dog, and all the other dogs defer to him. He still has his dignity, the best we can all hope for in our old age.

Laurie Wedler stayed on in the house, living with me for a while, then moved into Grande Prairie. She's spent the last two winters in Australia. She sold her dog, Call, and we're sitting her dog, Splash, for her.

This morning the gas lease road was freshly plowed of snow, and I was able to follow it on my power chair for over a kilometre into the muskeg northwest of home. I saw elk, moose, and fresh wolf tracks. The dogs were a bit nervous, which always makes me wonder if there are animals lurking in the heavy underbrush alongside the narrow road. I carry a bear-banger with me, in a case that's strapped behind my wheelchair seat, but I'm not sure how well I'd do at getting a banger threaded onto the firing mechanism if a critter was coming at me. Ideally, I'll never have to find out.

We're slowly building the cattle herd back up. Prices are higher now than they've ever been, but if they stay high at least ranchers will make a decent income for the work they do. We had to buy a new tractor and upgrade our haying equipment two years ago, and it's all our little farm can do to generate enough income to cover those payments. Jenny has taken over record keeping for the cattle, and she and Mat look after all the farm work. Jason is planning to come home and help us do some fencing this summer, on his vacation days. We sold most of our ewes so we could focus on our cattle herd, but we kept twenty sheep to have bucking stock for the Mutton Busting—kids' sheep riding—and for the herding demonstration in August at the Grovedale Fair. The sheep multi-task by serving as lawn mowers in the summer.

Ryon and Nicky Hemmingson gave us two mini-ponies last fall, Peewee and Studley. They're very quiet and well broken to drive. Ryon made a pony-drawn wagon that I can roll my power chair up onto. Learning to drive Studley and Peewee is one of my objectives once the weather gets warm enough. I also help out in the race office in July and August, during the Grande Prairie summer meet.

I've been doing some watercolour painting again, and Jenny's dad, Denis, made me some lovely wooden frames. I'll be donating my paintings for fundraisers, starting with the Grovedale Old Stars hockey tournament, where they have a silent auction to raise money to help people in need.

Percy will be five years old soon, and his little red-headed sister Emmalyn will soon be one. On the days Percy doesn't have pre-school at the country school his dad attended, or dance lessons in Grande Prairie, I hook the sleigh his Grandma Judy bought him for Christmas behind my power chair and put Emmy on my lap so the kids can come with me on my rounds of the farm. Mat has a job as one of the caretakers at the Grovedale hockey arena, and he works weekends there. Jenny has applied for a job at the Grande Prairie hospital. She'd like to nurse part-time once her maternity leave is up.

Jason and Christina got married two years ago, and they bought a house in Edmonton. Jay is the manager of global IT infrastructure for a lodging company, and Christina works for the provincial government. Over the last few years they've done some travelling, most recently to Vietnam, where they rented motorbikes and toured with friends. Their travelling may be curtailed somewhat now, though, since they've recently adopted a stray Heinz 57 dog named Clara.

Clara recently made her first visit to the farm, wearing her red tartan jacket and stylish boots. Needless to say, she caused quite a stir among the locals. Once she learned the ground rules and realized we were all one big happy family at the farm, she seemed to love it. The rest of us do too.

Acknowledgements

I HAVE A small handful of people to thank for helping me with the writing of this book, but I have a boatload to thank for helping me in the journey that led to it. I've been extremely fortunate to have mentors and friends who set an example of courage and strength. I am forever grateful.

Ultimately though, I would like to thank the folks who stood up for all of us when the chips were down because of Sandy's death. You cannot know how much it meant. That being said, the courage of the women who came forward to speak up for Mat by revealing Sandy's character, rises to the top of the list in my mind. I hope I do you all justice in my telling of the story.